SUCCESS through CRITICAL THINKING:

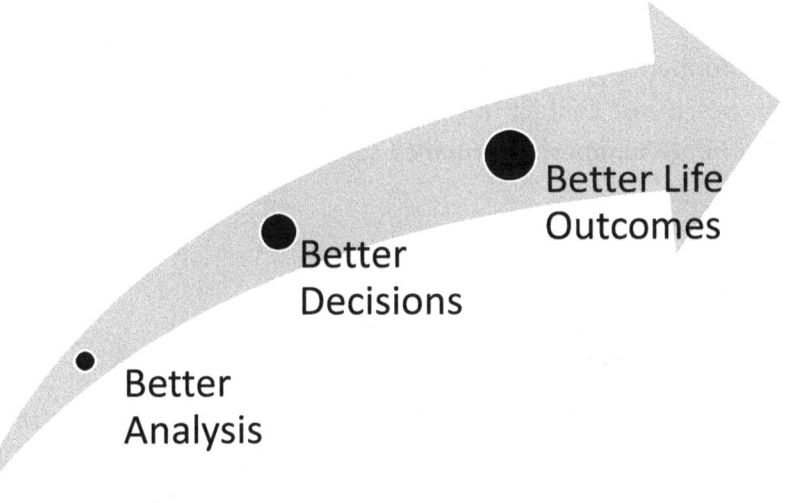

Creating a Launch Pad to Success – Part 1: From White Belt to Brown Belt

Wolfgang H. Hammes

Success through Critical Thinking

© Copyright 2019 by Wolfgang H. Hammes

All rights reserved. No part of this book may be reproduced in any form or by any electronic or mechanical means including information storage and retrieval systems without the permission in writing from the publisher, except by a reviewer, who may quote brief passages in a review.

Published by the Hammes Performance Improvement Group LLC

For information about permissions to reproduce selections of this book, please write to the publisher: The Hammes Performance Improvement Group, 4400 North Federal Highway, Suite 210-19, Boca Raton, FL 33431.

For information about hiring the author for workshops or keynote speeches, please contact The Hammes Performance Improvement Group LLC at **info@hammesperformance.com**

ISBN: 978-1-944614-02-7 (paperback)

LIMIT OF LIABILITY/DISCLAIMER OF WARRANTY: THE PUBLISHER AND THE AUTHOR MAKE NO REPRESENTATIONS OR WARRANTIES WITH RESPECT TO THE ACCURACY OR COMPLETENESS OF THE CONTENTS OF THE WORK AND SPECIFICALLY DISCLAIM ALL WARRANTIES, INCLUDING WITHOUT LIMITATION WARRANTIES OF FITNESS FOR A PARTICULAR PURPOSE. NO WARRANTY MAY BE CREATED OR EXTENDED BY SALES OR PROMOTIONAL MATERIALS. THE INFORMATION AND STRATEGIES CONTAINED HEREIN MAY NOT BE SUITABLE FOR EVERY SITUATION. THIS WORK IS DISTRIBUTED WITH THE UNDERSTANDING THAT NEITHER THE PUBLISHER NOR AUTHOR IS ENGAGED IN RENDERING LEGAL, ACCOUNTING, TAX, FINANCIAL, INVESTMENT, OR OTHER PROFESSIONAL SERVICES OR ADVICE. IF PROFESSIONAL ASSISTANCE IS REQUIRED, THE SERVICE OF A COMPETENT PROFESSIONAL PERSON SHOULD BE SOUGHT. NEITHER THE PUBLISHER NOR THE AUTHOR SHALL BE LIABLE FOR DAMAGES ARISING HEREFROM. THE FACT THAT AN ORGANIZATION OR WEBSITE IS REFERRED TO IN THIS WORK AS A CITATION AND/OR A POTENTIAL SOURCE OF FURTHER INFORMATION DOES NOT MEAN THAT THE AUTHOR OR THE PUBLISHER ENDORSES THE INFORMATION THE ORGANIZATION OR WEBSITE MAY PROVIDE OR RECOMMENDATIONS IT MAY MAKE.

To my parents

To my wife Angela and my children Claudia and Maximilian

PREFACE

This book has one objective: To make you more successful in life. How? By teaching you a skill that is one of the most powerful success enablers: Critical thinking.

Critical thinking has accompanied me throughout my life. Growing up in Germany provided me with a thorough education in critical thinking. Back then, critical thinking was a high priority. A lack of critical thinking led to disastrous and barbaric outcomes in Germany's history. Therefore, the urge to reflect critically on everything was almost excessive when I grew up. A common joke about Germans underlines this point: "What is the difference between Americans and Germans? Americans tend to think that every problem has got a solution while Germans tend to think that every solution has got a problem."

I was brought up being taught by my parents, relatives, and teachers to approach everything from a position of skepticism. Not to irritate others, but to avoid being manipulated or making suboptimal decisions.

My parents and grandparents taught me critical thinking at a young age. In school, my Latin, ancient Greek, and German literature classes introduced me to some of the greatest thinkers of the past. This solidified my foundation in critical thinking.

Later, at Trier University, the study of science theory and scientific method were integral parts of studying business administration. In short, my upbringing in Germany helped me build a solid foundation in critical thinking.

However, my breakthrough in critical thinking occurred when I joined the management consulting firm McKinsey & Company after the completion of my doctorate in business administration. I learned how to apply my theoretical knowledge of critical thinking to solve real-world business problems and to make clients more successful. I was amazed by the impressive results critical thinking can achieve. It led me to the belief that long-term success is not accidental, nor is failure. Both are consequences of the decisions we make and the actions that follow. In simple words, poor decisions lead to poor outcomes in life, good decisions lead to successful life outcomes. Therefore, improving decision-making processes should be the starting point for those who seek more success and better life outcomes. As you will learn in this book, critical thinking is the most effective and efficient tool to accomplish this. I call this the Critical Thinking Success Chain; better analysis leads to better decisions, which then leads to better life outcomes.

Unfortunately, this simple concept is underused in today's world. Most people make important decisions without thorough analysis and thoughtful reflection. We follow (uncritically) the herd, we let ourselves be manipulated by advertisements and sales pitches, or, even worse, we outsource our decision-making processes to so-called experts, gurus, and organizations whose incentives are clearly not aligned with ours. By doing so we accept suboptimal outcomes in life. In the worst case, we allow others to take advantage of us.

This raises an important question: If critical thinking is so powerful and so important for our long-term success, why don't we use it more consistently? The answer is simple. First, critical thinking is hard work. The analytic work required for making good decisions can be cumbersome and time-intensive. Second, past successes often make us overly confident, arrogant, and complacent. We feel comfortable skipping critical thinking and jumping to a decision without doing proper analysis first. Third, and perhaps most important, we are seduced by an alternative approach that appears to be less cumbersome: positive thinking.

Critical thinking and positive thinking are opposing ends of a continuum. They are not compatible with each other. Positive thinking encourages an (unjustified) expectation of positive outcomes. Worrying about adverse future developments, risks, and uncertainties is actively discouraged. "Don't worry" is the famous battle cry of the positive thinking movement.

Positive thinking is built on a biased perception of the world and future outcomes. In the short term, it makes us feel good. Maybe this explains the increasing popularity of the concept. In the long term, however, it almost always leads to dangerous unpreparedness, less effort in our work, and exaggerated levels of optimism. Becoming a "Happy Underachiever" is often the result of positive thinking.

Critical thinking works differently. Initial worrying encourages thorough analysis of a problem. This analysis is likely to lead to high quality decision making and outstanding preparedness. Both are prerequisites to long-term success and to continually outperform. In other words, instead of becoming a *happy loser*, you are more likely to become a *worried overachiever*.

In today's world, critical thinking is used less and less. You are much more likely to hear "don't worry, it is going to be fine" than "think critically." We often observe politicians, business people, investors, regulators, and the general public making material decisions based on opinions, unproven beliefs, ideologies, and self-interest and not on rigorous fact-based analyses. This is a worrisome development.

I wrote this book to start a renaissance of critical thinking. More specifically, to teach critical thinking tools and approaches that can be applied easily in everyday life. The more people follow the Critical Thinking Success Chain (i.e., better analysis, better decisions, better life outcomes), the better the results will be for both individuals and society.

This book consists of a sequence of practical lessons that build on each other. Many of the concepts, ideas, and frameworks are based on my own life experiences. From martial arts, I adopted the concept of different colored belts to mark the progression in learning. Step by step, or belt by belt, you will learn new frameworks, concepts, and ideas. At the end of each chapter, I have included a series of real-world exercises that help you apply theoretical knowledge to practical issues.

The focus of this book is on the foundation of critical thinking (i.e., white belt to brown belt). The next book, "*Success through Critical Thinking Part Two – The Black Belt Classes*" will focus on more advanced topics. Chapter 10 allows you to take a peek at some of the topics discussed in the black belt classes.

Again, this is a practical book. There are many great books available on the theoretical foundations of critical thinking. For anyone interested in the theoretical groundwork, I recommend studying the works and ideas of ancient Greek philosophers (e.g., Socrates, Plato, Aristotle), famous science theorists (e.g., Karl Popper), or other exceptional thinkers (e.g., Immanuel Kant on Enlightenment).

I personally like to examine the works of thinkers from different times and circumstances. For example, one can get great inspiration from the works of Johann Wolfgang von Goethe (e.g., *Faust I & II*) as well as thinkers of the twentieth century such as Paul Watzlawick. Thanks to modern technology, these works are available to you at little cost and effort. Not using the immensely valuable insights of these great thinkers would be a terrible waste.[1]

There is much discussion about how to make books gender neutral. When writing, I strove to make this book easy to read. I only used gender specific terms for that purpose (e.g., "he" instead of "he/she").

I close by thanking the reader for the purchase of this book. I am honored that you chose me as one of your guides for exploring this important topic. Becoming a critical thinker is a life-changing journey and I wish you great luck in this endeavor.

Dr. Wolfgang Hammes

Boca Raton, Florida

Table of Contents

PREFACE 5

INTRODUCTION: THE CONNECTION BETWEEN CRITICAL THINKING AND LONG-TERM SUCCESS 15

PART I: LEARNING THE BASICS 27

CHAPTER 1 - THE WHITE BELT: WHAT IS CRITICAL THINKING? – MOVING FROM AN *"I GUESS WORLD"* TO AN *"I KNOW WORLD"* 28

CHAPTER 2 - THE YELLOW BELT: THE FIRST FIVE STEPS ON YOUR JOURNEY TO BECOMING A BLACK BELT IN CRITICAL THINKING 38

CHAPTER 3 -THE ORANGE BELT: THE FOUR PRAGMATIC NAVIGATION POINTS FOR CRITICAL THINKING 58

CHAPTER 4 - THE GREEN BELT: LEVERAGE CRITICAL THINKING TO ACHIEVE A STATE OF TOTAL STRATEGIC PREPAREDNESS 75

CHAPTER 5 - THE BLUE BELT: DIFFERENT PROBLEMS REQUIRE DIFFERENT APPROACHES TO THINKING 99

EXCURSUS: HOW CRITICAL THINKING IMPACTS YOUR HAPPINESS AND SOCIAL LIFE 123

PART II: PREPARING FOR MASTER LEVEL (THE BROWN BELT CLASSES): SUCCESSFULLY DEALING WITH AN INCREASINGLY IRRATIONAL WORLD 133

CHAPTER 6 - THE BROWN BELT: A CRISIS OF REASONING. HOW AN IRRATIONAL WORLD CHALLENGES CRITICAL THINKERS 134

CHAPTER 7 - THE BROWN BELT: HOW CRITICAL THINKERS CAN TURN WIDESPREAD IRRATIONALITY INTO FORTUNES 145

CHAPTER 8 - THE BROWN BELT: THE POWER OF CRITICAL OBSERVATION 159

PART III: A LOOK AHEAD TO THE BLACKBELT CLASSES AND NEXT STEPS 173

CHAPTER 9: LOOKING AHEAD TO BLACK BELT CLASSES 174

CHAPTER 10: CONCLUSION AND NEXT STEPS 186

FOOTNOTES 189

BIBLIOGRAPHY 195

ACKNOWLEDGMENTS 197

ABOUT THE AUTHOR 199

ABOUT THE HAMMES PERFORMANCE IMPROVEMENT GROUP LLC 201

OTHER BOOKS BY THE AUTHOR 203

INTRODUCTION: THE CONNECTION BETWEEN CRITICAL THINKING AND LONG-TERM SUCCESS

Long-term success is not accidental and neither is failure. This is the most important conclusion from my lifelong fascination with the study of success and failure. It is mainly we, or more specifically, our decisions and actions that greatly determine our life outcomes. Therefore, the starting point for becoming more successful in life is making better decisions. One skill is indispensable for doing so: critical thinking. Let me explain this important topic in more detail.

Since childhood, I have been fascinated by the question of what makes a person or a team successful and others not. As a young boy, I tried to predict and explain the success of soccer stars and teams. What makes the difference between successful and less successful soccer players, coaches, and teams? Why can't the unsuccessful teams (including my favored team) simply copy the more successful teams to become equally successful?

Later, my research interest in explaining success and failure widened to include business, politics, arts, and other aspects of life. The questions that captured my interest included a wide spectrum: Why do some companies outperform others for long periods of time? Why do some countries seem to get stuck in chaos or mediocrity while others succeed for extended periods? Why has no superpower survived in world history?

The breakthrough of my research came through my professional work as a management consultant and later as an investment banker. I had the privilege to work closely with highly successful individuals and companies. This enabled me to gain a direct and detailed understanding of their conduct. I was no longer dependent on other people's observations and interpretations on what makes people and organizations successful. Instead, I could observe successful individuals and organizations first hand and compare their conduct with that of less successful ones. Let me add that more often than not my observations on success and failure were fundamentally different from those shared in bestselling books and magazine articles.

As part of a research project, I selected a group of highly successful people with whom I had worked closely enough to assess realistically the drivers of their success. The people in this sample were long-term successful overachievers. They appeared to be successful no matter what they did. They could switch careers and employers and work in different countries and cultures and they would continue to be highly successful. I call these people *Super Performers* (see chart 1 for a more detailed description). An in-depth description of their secrets to success will be the subject of another book.

Chart 1: Criteria for being a *Super Performer*

CRITERIA FOR BEING A *SUPER PERFORMER*
• Successful on their own; no significant help by others (e.g., rich, connected parents) • Long-term success (no "one-hit wonders") • Success in different careers and different arenas (e.g., a great athlete becoming successful in business; a business person who has long-term success in different companies, jobs, and countries) • I know them well enough to verify their success story

I scrutinized their upbringing, education, conduct, decision-making processes, and behavior. In short, I looked at every possible factor that could explain their long-term overachievement.

The results were eye opening and confirmed my hypothesis that long-term success was not accidental, but the result of specific conduct, sophisticated strategies, and targeted actions. What surprised me was that there was one dominant commonality among all *Super Performers*: They all were "black belts" in critical thinking. For decades their lives were guided by an unconditional dedication to critical thinking. There was no important decision to be made that was not preceded by an intense period of critical thinking and rigorous, fact-based analysis. It was not talent, luck, or intuition that guided their decision making. It was a rigorous and consistent commitment to critical thinking.

Critical thinking is a term that is widely used and very loosely defined. Almost every management job description states critical thinking as a required skill. But how *Super Performers* employ critical thinking is different. It can be best described as a zest for avoidance of guessing and hoping and instead as an unconditional commitment to the world of knowledge and understanding. This is the key difference between those who practice critical thinking and those who do not. Therefore, I define critical thinking in this book as the process of moving from an *"I guess world"* to an *"I know world."*

There is a fundamental difference between the two worlds. In the first, suboptimal decisions are made based on insufficient, superficial, incomplete, or even wrong analysis (i.e., guesses). In some extreme cases, decisions are made in the complete absence of analysis. These are "gut decisions." Not surprisingly, the lack of critical thinking leads to lower quality decisions and suboptimal outcomes in life.

Unfortunately, most of modern society's decision making takes place in the *I guess world*. Although most of us could easily move to the *I know world*, few actually do. This becomes apparent when we look at our daily decision making.

For example, almost everyone pursues the goal of a healthy and pain free life. In fact, most people I know would rate good health/absence of pain as one of their top two goals. However, our decision making regarding good health seems to be firmly anchored in the *I guess world*. We spend very little time and effort to determine analytically what is best for our health. Consequently, our decisions regarding food intake are not the result of rigorous critical thinking aimed at linking analysis and goals to daily decision making. Instead, we make poor decisions regarding our nutrition and lifestyle choices leading to a situation of being "overfed and undernourished."[2] Our poor decisions sabotage one of our most important goals.

The same is true for most other aspects of our personal and professional lives. We operate mostly in an *I guess world*. In this world, superficial thinking prevails over critical thinking. As a result, suboptimal decisions are made constantly. This prevents us from reaching our true potential.

The *Super Performers* that I studied behave differently. They live in the *I know world* and they do not want to leave it. They know that critical thinking is a powerful instrument for decision making and they also know that better decisions lead to dramatically better outcomes. They follow the Critical Thinking Success Chain illustrated in chart 2 to the greatest extent possible.

Chart 2: The Critical Thinking Success Chain

Better Analysis → Better Decisions → Better Outcomes

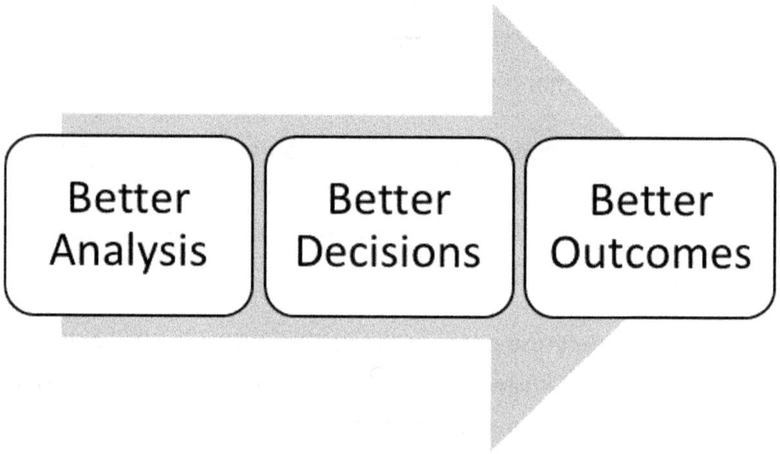

Super Performers never make important decisions without conducting diligent analysis. Critical thinking plays a decisive role on this path from analysis to decisions to outcomes.

Once you align your life's decision making with the critical thinking success chain, two things will change. First, you will make fewer mistakes as your decisions are no longer based on guesses, but on fact-based analysis. The quality of your decisions will improve quite significantly.

Second, you will achieve a better state of preparedness. As we learn in chapter four, high levels of preparedness are key to becoming and staying successful in the long term. You are less likely to be caught unprepared when risks and opportunities cross your path. Preparedness not only protects you from risks and disruptions. It can also enable you to turn risks into attractive opportunities, enabling you to outperform your less prepared peer group.

The difference between living in the *I guess world* and the *I know world* can be significant as the financial crisis of 2007 clearly illustrates. During the early 2000s, millions of Americans believed that investments in U.S. residential real estate were winning strategies with little risk. Most formed their convictions about the prospects of the U.S. housing market by extrapolating recent trends into the future, not on fact-based analysis of demographics, sustainability of debt leverage, and other criteria affecting housing prices.

A handful of hedge fund managers engaged in rigorous critical thinking to challenge the assumptions shared by the majority of market participants. They quickly realized that the assumptions on which trillions of dollars were invested in real estate and related securities (e.g., mortgage bonds, CLOs) were unfounded. In fact, investors and financial institutions created a fragile house of cards that would likely collapse in the near future.

Eventually, the scenario anticipated by critical thinkers materialized and the financial industry slid into one of the worst crises in modern financial history. When the financial crisis of 2007 unfolded, the hedge fund managers from the *I know world* made fortunes, while the people from the *I guess world* lost fortunes.

Once the critical thinking success chain is broken, long-term success is hard to obtain. It is close to impossible to obtain great outcomes when making, at best, average decisions. It exemplifies the well-known "garbage in, garbage out" principle.

When I work with clients, I always encourage them to make critical thinking the centerpiece of all of their decision making. This requires a great deal of training. For this purpose, I developed a *Four Factor Critical Thinking Success Model* that helps link the important success drivers of strategy, risk management, and future anticipation with critical thinking (see chart 3). This framework can be used by both organizations and individuals. It is important to note that critical thinking sits at the center of this model.

Chart 3: The *Four Factor Critical Thinking Success Model*

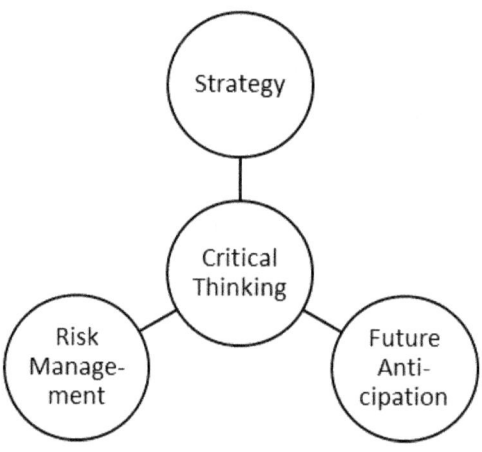

Critical thinking is not only a business tool. Every aspect of life profits from well-practiced critical thinking. Critical thinking can help improve athletic performance, address medical and health related issues, and solve challenging personal problems. In fact, my wife and I used critical thinking when addressing complex medical issues for one of our children.

Many books about critical thinking are highly theoretical and discuss complex issues in science theory. While these books are important to cement the theoretical foundation of critical thinking, they are of limited use in daily decision making. This book focuses on practical decisions in everyday life. My goal is to provide applicable ideas and concepts that will help you make better decisions and achieve better outcomes. In short, my goal is to make you more successful.

My approach to critical thinking unites five different ambitions for critical thinking as shown in chart 4. I refer to this approach as the PRACT model of critical thinking.

Chart 4: The PRACT Model of Critical Thinking

CRITICAL THINKING AMBITIONS	
Practical	• Focus on achieving better outcomes in life; usable in everyday life
Relevant	• Application of critical thinking to relevant and important topics, not inconsequential, trivial topics
Applied	• Applied to real situations, not theoretical discussions
Constructive	• Embrace constructive skepticism: being difficult is not the same as being constructively critical
Thinking	• Thinking instead of guessing

Despite the enormous potential for creating better outcomes for both the individual and society, critical thinking is greatly neglected. Few schools make it a stand-alone topic in their curriculums. Few U.S. business schools make critical thinking a mandatory class taught by experienced professionals (although almost all business schools claim to teach the skill). Corporations also often neglect this topic. I personally think that most large corporations would benefit from a stand-alone critical thinking department that independently analyzes the soundness of strategies pursued, preparedness for potential risks and disruptions, and the wide spectrum of potential future scenarios and outcomes.

The neglect of critical thinking is good news for experienced critical thinkers. In an *I guess world* environment, critical thinkers can achieve outsized returns by practicing their skills. They outsmart their competitors. In the world of investments, we can see this clearly. Top investors are often black belts in critical thinking. For example, famous hedge fund manager George Soros has become an expert in science theory, the academic foundation of critical thinking, and has written extensively about the work of science theorist Karl Popper and the theory of scientific method.[3]

The academic discipline of science theory provides very useful concepts and tools for critical thinking. Unfortunately, most of today's students, both undergraduate and graduate, leave their universities without having been exposed to this field. Also, the insights of great philosophers such as Socrates, Plato, and Aristotle remain unknown to many college graduates. Obviously, these education deficits do not encourage and spread critical thinking.

HOW TO USE THIS BOOK

The goal of this book is to get you started on your journey to a black belt in critical thinking. As in martial arts, progress toward a black belt requires both studying and practicing the techniques.

The discipline of critical thinking can sometimes be confusing to novices. Therefore, I structured this book as a class that you take at your own speed. I used the belt system from martial arts to organize the educational path from being a novice to becoming an expert critical thinker.

Each chapter (i.e., each belt color) introduces a new set of tools, concepts, and ideas, followed by a set of exercises to apply theory to practice. Once you have finished both theory and practice, you are awarded a new belt.

This book focuses on the foundation of critical thinking. You start with the white belt techniques and move up to the advanced level (i.e., brown belt classes). The next book, "*Success through Critical Thinking Part Two – The Blackbelt Classes,*" will introduce the black belt classes. These lessons aim to make you a black belt of critical thinking, the destination of our journey.

A word of caution: Even after you have achieved black belt status in critical thinking, the journey must continue. We should never relax our critical thinking standards nor should we stop acquiring new critical thinking skills. There are too many examples of individuals, teams, and organizations that suffered spectacular failures after extended periods of success. These failures are similar to the fate of Icarus in Greek mythology. Keep in mind that having success is likely to be your biggest risk factor going forward. We will talk about this in more detail in the black belt classes. Success makes us complacent, overconfident, negligent, and uncritical. These are attitudes incompatible with the requirements of critical thinking and long-term success.

Critical thinking is the key tool that helped me achieve professional and personal outcomes beyond my wildest imagination. I sincerely hope that you have similar positive experiences. Thank you for choosing my book to learn this important skill and good luck on your journey to becoming a black belt in critical thinking.

Summary:

In this chapter, the following tools, frameworks, and concepts are discussed:

- *Critical Thinking Success Chain*: Better Analysis, Better Decisions, Better Outcomes
- *I guess world* versus *I know world*
- *Super Performers* (Criteria)
- *Four Factor Critical Thinking Success Model* (Critical thinking, strategy, risk management, and future anticipation)
- *PRACT Model of Critical Thinking* (Practical Relevant Applied Constructive Thinking)

PART I: LEARNING THE BASICS

CHAPTER 1 - THE WHITE BELT: WHAT IS CRITICAL THINKING? – MOVING FROM AN "*I GUESS WORLD*" TO AN "*I KNOW WORLD*"

When you ask a company for the key competencies they are looking for when hiring new employees, critical thinking is likely to top the list. Critical thinkers are in high demand.

But what is critical thinking? How can we define it in a practical manner? Surprisingly, there is great confusion about what critical thinking is. Ask people to define critical thinking and you are likely to encounter either silence or a sequence of vague descriptions, examples, and anecdotes. In the academic world, there are lengthy, complicated attempts to define critical thinking that provide little help for people who seek to make better decisions and to achieve better outcomes in their daily lives. We need a simple and practical definition that warns us whenever we leave the path of critical thinking.

Simply being difficult and destructive in a team session does not constitute critical thinking. Similarly, questioning everything without the intention of making better decisions or seeking better outcomes is destructive behavior that has nothing to do with critical thinking.

For this book, I have created a simple yet powerful definition of critical thinking: *Critical thinking is the cognitive process of moving from an "I guess world" to an "I know world."* In this context, "I know" refers to both the things we know and the things we know that we do not know (that is, uncertain situations).

My definition of critical thinking is a reflection of my professional experience as a management consultant. I cannot count the number of times managers proposed important strategic moves based on guesses derived from insufficient and superficial analysis. Such conduct leaves us in the *I guess world*, a dangerous place when making consequential decisions.

It is equally dangerous to base important decisions on incorrect beliefs. For example, prior to the financial crisis of 2007, top managers of many financial institutions wrongly believed that their risk exposure and risk management capabilities were in line with their risk appetites and required standards. They failed to understand the real risk exposure they had accumulated. Most managers and investors were living in the *I guess world* of doing business.

If they had engaged in rigorous critical thinking (as a handful of sophisticated hedge fund managers did),[4] they would have understood their dangerous risk management shortcomings, which would have enabled them to rectify the situation. They took a pass at moving from the *I guess world* to the *I know world* and suffered terrible consequences while the handful of hedge fund managers who employed critical thinking and correctly identified enormous risk management deficits made fortunes.

Simple critical thinking tools and concepts such as stress-testing our beliefs, key models, and assumptions, conducting scenario analyses of potential outcomes, or creating strategic risk radar screens would have enabled managers of financial institutions to see the real world.

There is a huge difference between guessing and knowing. Often, this difference explains why some people, teams, and organizations are winners and others not. People in the *I guess world* set themselves up for suboptimal results. They are constantly in a state of unpreparedness for situations that deviate from their guesses.

My definition of critical thinking may sound overly simplistic, but it is extremely powerful. Most people are unaware of how many of their decisions are the result of living in the *I guess world*. In training sessions, I challenge people to review past situations in their lives that led to suboptimal results. In most cases, we can link these suboptimal outcomes to faulty or superficial analyses prior to making material decisions. This is symptomatic of being anchored in the *I guess world*.

If we always ask ourselves whether our decisions were derived by guessing or knowing (and ensure that the latter is the case), we are likely to improve dramatically the quality of our decisions, which will lead to vastly improved life outcomes. A simple move from guessing to knowing will make all the difference.

For example, you do not want your doctor to guess when recommending surgery or prescribing medication with potentially serious side effects. You want your doctor to have done exhaustive and rigorous analyses before arriving at a conclusion. Similarly, you do not want to be in the *I guess world* when you make a big investment decision such as buying a house. You should do everything possible to move from *I guess* to *I know*. There are many ways to accomplish this. You can access the knowledge of specialists (e.g., property appraiser, mold inspector, construction professional) to assess a property. You can research the neighborhood's pricing trends, crime rates, environmental issues, and planned infrastructure changes (e.g., new building projects, new bus or train lines). Moving to the *I know world* does not require rocket science, but it does call for some analytical work to be done.

Chart 5: Comparing the *I guess world* to the *I know world*

I guess world	*I know world*
• Suboptimal decisions and outcomes • Risk of unpreparedness for adverse developments • Faster, less work intensive (the lazy way) • In the future: Extra time and costs fixing past mistakes	• Better decisions lead to better outcomes in the long term • High degree of preparedness for risks and new opportunities • Time intensive, slower decision-making processes

Unfortunately, the majority of decisions made in our personal and professional lives tend to be the product of the *I guess world*. In most cases, laziness, passivity, perceived time pressure, and political considerations are to blame for this unsatisfactory situation. Many are not even aware that they live in the *I guess world*. They wonder why others continue to be more successful than they. They blame their lack of success on unfair treatment, bad luck, or fate, while the key to becoming more successful is readily available. They need to engage unconditionally in critical thinking and move from the *I guess world* of making decisions to the *I know world*. It sounds simple and with a little practice it will be simple. But many people refuse to take this step.

To avoid the perilous traps of the *I guess world*, many tools and concepts are available. One of the first steps is to watch out for words and phrases that clearly indicate uncritical thinking (see chart 6). If you hear any of these words or phrases, activate your critical thinking defense mechanism immediately.

Chart 6: Words and phrases that expose uncritical thinkers from the *I guess world*

Words and phrases from the *I guess world*	
• I guess	• Rough estimate
• I believe	• Don't worry, it will be fine
• I think	• Nobody knows …
• I did a back of the envelope calculation	• Too much analysis leads to paralysis … let's move on
• I did a quick and dirty analysis of the problem	• This time is different
	• Trust me …
• I am pretty sure that …	• Everybody else does it …

It is shocking how often our critical thinking defense mechanism remains inactive as we blindly follow others' suggestions. For me, this is the reason why *fake news* has become such a big problem. In a world of critical thinking, *fake news* would not be a serious issue as proper fact-based analysis (including credibility checks of authors and sources) would be second nature and would always precede any decision-making processes.

The biggest problem in decision making is that in the short- and mid-term, we often get away with guessing and not knowing. In fact, following the herd when making investment decisions can be a profitable strategy in the short- and even mid-term, as we can witness during the build-up stage of financial bubbles. Herd mentality can create a strong, reinforcing momentum that keeps prices going up and illusions alive. However, when markets turn, it is the critical thinkers who are prepared to deal with the consequences.

In 2007, I hoped that the financial crisis would spark a renaissance of critical thinking. It became brutally obvious that being in the *I guess world* led to an economic and financial crisis that took us close to the abyss. But my hopes were not realized. We simply failed to learn our lessons. Excessive debt leverage, which was blamed for the severe economic, financial, and social disruptions during the financial crisis of 2007, reached new record levels. The argument that "this time is different" should be a flashing red warning for every critical thinker. But the lack of critical thinking is responsible for most people not noticing these warning signs.

A deficit of critical thinking seems to be a particular issue for young people, as the following anecdote illustrates. The clash between old and new school thinking cannot be better described than in this example.

Business Anecdote:

A young management consultant from a prestigious U.S. business school was presenting strategic recommendations to an experienced German top manager. The manger was not immediately convinced by the radical recommendations presented to him by the young, fast-talking consultant. He asked for the analytical foundation of the recommendations.

The young consultant referred to several "back of the envelope" calculations he did before coming to his recommendations for the client.

He failed to understand that to a nonnative English speaker, "back of the envelope" sounded like the opposite of a rigorous analysis. This was upsetting to the manager when confronted with very radical strategic recommendations.

> *Not surprisingly, the manager interrupted the presentation and asked the consultant to come back when his analysis was expanded from the back of an envelope to several pieces of standard paper.*

Success is a direct consequence of how good our decisions are. If our decisions are based on superficial and uncritical analysis, we will be less successful in the long term. We may get away with it for months or even years during benign economic circumstances. However, eventually the tide will go out and reveal who was swimming naked (i.e., not using critical thinking).

Compromising the analyses that precede our decisions is like building a house on a weak foundation. It is an unacceptable proposition for anyone who is seriously interested in better outcomes. We therefore must anchor our decision making firmly in the *I know world*, as chart 7 illustrates.

Chart 7: Decision making in an *I guess world* versus an *I know world*

I guess world	*I know world*
• Linear extrapolation of past trends • Follow conventional wisdom and established practices • Follow others without due diligence checks • Superficial analysis that lacks depth, scope, completeness, or time horizon • Use of unverified data • Unwilling to change or revise decisions, even if new data or reasoning raise doubts about conclusions • Unwilling to test hypotheses and beliefs	• Attitude of constructive skepticism when it comes to trends, assumptions, established practices, and decision making • Personally conduct in-depth, fact-based, complete analysis • Verification of data sources • Never rush into important decisions • Open to change/revise decisions when new facts become available • Willing to question and challenge own hypotheses and beliefs

Critical thinking starts with an attitude of constructive skepticism (see chart 8). This is distinctively different from a competing approach, positive thinking.

When you become a critical thinker, you will be confronted hundreds of times with the dangerously naïve battle cry of the positive thinking movement: "Don't worry, it is going to be fine." In my view, positive thinking is dangerous. It puts you at risk of being unprepared for scenarios and outcomes that deviate from the expected path. Positive thinking assumes positive outcomes in the future. As a result, the positive thinker is less motivated, due to his biased view of the future, to prepare for potential risks, uncertainties, or adverse developments.

Critical thinking seeks to avoid such unpreparedness by adopting the attitude of constructive skepticism, which takes a neutral and more balanced view of future developments. A critical thinker is happy when the future is blessed with benign outcomes, but he is also prepared to deal with adverse developments (see chart 8).

I discuss the perils of positive thinking in more detail later. At this point of your journey, note that positive thinking and critical thinking are two incompatible approaches to seeking better outcomes. Positive thinking may make you feel better, but it is critical thinking that brings long-term success and fulfillment.

Chart 8: Constructive skepticism: The key to critical thinking

CONSTRUCTIVE SKEPTICISM	
What it is:	• An insistence on rigorous and thorough analysis • A constructive attitude to differentiate between truth and beliefs, facts and myths • A protective mechanism to prevent approving insufficiently analyzed recommendations
What it is not:	• Being difficult or unreasonable • Attacking or insulting others • An excuse for dysfunctional behavior

It is important that skepticism is used in a constructive manner. The goal is not to be difficult or confrontational. Such behavior is destructive and dysfunctional. Critical thinking should never be used to insult others or to sabotage discussion. The goal is to achieve better outcomes, not to engage in useless fighting.

At the end of this chapter, I highlight the enormous importance of understanding the difference between living in an *I guess world* versus an *I know world*. Understanding this difference and acting on it is not just a key requirement for becoming a critical thinker. It is the basis for long-term success. Living in an *I know world* enables us to better understand and manage risks (keep in mind that risks for which we are unprepared are the biggest impediments to success) and exploit attractive opportunities in a safer way.

Summary:

In this chapter, the following tools, frameworks, and concepts are discussed:

- *I guess world* (superficial thinking) versus *I know world* (critical thinking)
- *Constructive skepticism*
- Positive thinking versus critical thinking
- The problem of *fake news*

Exercises

1. In your next business meeting or discussion with friends, take note of how many words or phrases are used that indicate being in the *I guess world* of uncritical thinking (see chart 6).
2. Observe people you work with or know well. Assign them to the *I guess world* or the *I know world* category. In which group do you find more long-term successful people?
3. Analyze examples of past successes and failures in your life. How often were past failures linked to issues of the *I guess world* and how often were successes linked to being in the *I know world*?

Congratulations! If you have carefully reflected on this chapter and conducted the suggested exercises, you have met the requirements for the white belt in critical thinking. We now move on to earning the yellow belt.

CHAPTER 2 - THE YELLOW BELT: THE FIRST FIVE STEPS ON YOUR JOURNEY TO BECOMING A BLACK BELT IN CRITICAL THINKING

The Chinese philosopher Lao Tzu once wrote: "A journey of a thousand miles begins with a single step."[5] The same is true for our becoming experts in critical thinking. The most important activity of this journey is the first step. This must be a conscious decision to leave the world of rushed and suboptimal decisions behind. You are starting a journey that seeks to trade guessing for knowing and, as a result, swap mediocrity for long-term success. Once the first step is taken, the next thousand steps tend to follow almost automatically.

To start your journey, I suggest the following five initial steps (see chart 9). You can use these five steps as your critical thinking starter program. Successfully implementing this five-step program will earn you a yellow belt in critical thinking and will provide you with the momentum and motivation to continue your journey to earning a black belt.

Chart 9: The five initial steps to becoming a critical thinker

FIVE INITIAL STEPS TO BECOMING A CRITICAL THINKER
Step 1: Practice constructive skepticism
Step 2: Pack your backpack for a successful journey (the things you need)
Step 3: Remove items from your backpack (the things that hold you back)
Step 4: Ban these words from your vocabulary
Step 5: Build a network of people who challenge your views

STEP 1: PRACTICE CONSTRUCTIVE SKEPTICISM

In the previous chapter, I discussed briefly the importance of adopting a new attitude to enable transformation into critical thinkers, constructive skepticism. Before we change anything else about our lives, we need to make this first step.

In the introduction to this book, I mention my research on people whom I call *Super Performers*. This group consists of people who have consistently performed at the highest levels and achieved success in different settings (e.g., countries, careers, fields). I know them quite well and this allows me to analyze their secrets of success first hand. I do not have to rely on possibly inaccurate secondary sources.

There are two crucial differences between *Super Performers* and average performers. First, *Super Performers* are black belts in critical thinking. Second, and this is a bit surprising for many believers in the power of positive thinking, they are anything but positive thinkers. In fact, their conduct is based on what I described in the previous chapter as the attitude of constructive skepticism. They do not assume that the future will be filled with positive outcomes. Also, they do not naively follow a suggestion or recommendation without demanding to see the evidence on which it is based. They are hesitant to adopt new fads and fashions. They remain stubbornly undecided and reluctant to act until sufficient evidence has been collected to justify a new decision or action.

Constructive skepticism means taking responsibility for one's own outcomes by demanding meaningful analysis before making consequential decisions. As a result, the quality of *Super Performers'* decisions tends to be substantially higher than that of those made by average performers. This is the true secret to their long-term success.

> **Quick Exercise: Constructive skepticism**
>
> Select five consequential decisions you have made that did not achieve the success you sought (e.g., professional career, investment, finance, or health-related). Assess how much analysis preceded the decision making. Then, assess your state of mind and attitude when making those poor decisions. Which of the following best describes you when making the decisions: positive thinking, distracted, enthusiastic, following the herd, or constructively skeptical? Discuss what would have happened if you had been in a state of constructive skepticism when making those poor decisions.

Constructive skepticism is a protective mechanism against suboptimal analysis, which will almost certainly lead to inferior decision making and poor outcomes.

People who practice constructive skepticism do not jump to conclusions. Instead, they ask a lot of questions, challenge arguments, and probe the analytic rigor of conclusions presented to them. All these activities are conducted with a constructive mindset that seeks to be part of the team finding optimum solutions. Chart 10 offers sample questions that can help you become a constructive skeptic.

Chart 10: Sample questions for constructive skeptics

SAMPLE QUESTIONS TO APPLY CONSTRUCTIVE SKEPTICISM
• What is the factual or empirical evidence for the position or recommendation presented to you? • What analyses have been done to support a position or recommendation presented to you? Is the quality of the research sufficiently high? • Are there any counterexamples that suggest the position or recommendation is not acceptable (so-called black swans)? • What could go wrong if you accept the position or recommendation being presented? What are likely risks? What are the worst possible risks? Are you comfortable with these risks? • Is the person presenting the position or recommendation independent, credible, free of conflicting interests?

First, a caveat. At the beginning, it can be quite difficult to be a constructive skeptic. Not only does the widespread belief in positive thinking present challenging issues, but our obsession with speed is equally challenging. The modern world wrongly believes that fast decision making and speedy implementation is better than thorough, slower decision making. Therefore, your environment will pressure you to react swiftly to proposals and recommendations. In business meetings, it can be challenging when you are the only one who voices doubt about the analytical rigor of a recommendation. Substantial social pressure can emerge when a constructive skeptic blocks decision-making processes due to a demand for more convincing evidence.

How can you deal with such pressure when you are surrounded by speed obsessed colleagues? The group of *Super Performers* I studied has a very simple recipe to deal with such situations. They simply ignore time pressure put on them. Even if there are twenty people in the room and everyone else has already approved a recommendation and is eager to move on, they will stoically take as much time as they need to make a good decision. They will not back material decisions that are based on insufficient or faulty evidence. Initially, this is difficult for a novice critical thinker. However, with practice (and backed by initial success), you will gain the courage and assertiveness to continue.

> **Recommendation for better understanding the power of *effective slowness*:**
>
> In the black belt classes, we will discuss in more detail the need for an appropriate speed when making decisions (i.e., *effective slowness*). In the meantime, you may find some inspiration on the power of slowness in the following two sources. First, Sten Nadolny's book *The Discovery of Slowness* recounts the story of Arctic explorer Sir John Franklin and how he manages to turn slowness into a competitive weapon. Second, the movie *Twelve Angry Men* describes brilliantly how slowing down the decision-making process of a jury uncovers new material evidence that leads to a reversal of the initial majority view and the discovery of truth.

Super Performers never allow others to rush them. In fact, they can get quite upset and angry if someone tries to do so. Their behavior has served them well and you should copy it.

STEP 2: PACK YOUR BACKPACK FOR A SUCCESSFUL JOURNEY

After adopting the attitude of a constructive skeptic, you need to start packing your backpack for the journey. Like a mountain climber who needs the right equipment and provisions for a challenging climb, you need to select the right tools, concepts, and mental frameworks for your journey.

Chart 11 presents some ideas of what you may put into your backpack. The good thing about this journey is that at any point you can revise your decisions and change the contents. This might be necessary as you face different environments and circumstances. These specific situations will ultimately determine which concepts and tools are needed. A trip to a challenging mountain in the Himalayas requires a different backpack than a weekend hike up a local mountain. Therefore, chart 11 illustrates the starter backpack for aspiring critical thinkers. You will change it over time, but for now the following tools and concepts may be sufficient.

Chart 11: Pack your backpack for the start of your journey

WHAT YOU NEED TO HAVE IN YOUR BACKPACK	
<ul><li>Open-mindedness</li><li>Constructive skepticism</li><li>Zest to ask questions until you get to the bottom of things</li><li>Courage to challenge others (including leaders) and to say no</li><li>Time</li><li>Interdisciplinary thinking</li><li>Stress management techniques (for individuals and teams)</li></ul>	<ul><li>Fact-based analysis</li><li>Willingness to look at issues from different perspectives</li><li>The mindset of an engineer (decompose and reconfigure complex issues)</li><li>Willingness to learn from past mistakes</li><li>Patience</li><li>Ambition</li><li>Humor[6]</li><li>Team management skills</li><li>Healthy lifestyle</li></ul>

While everything listed is important, I would like to highlight one in particular, open-mindedness. Most people, teams, and organizations are trapped in their traditions, rituals, conventions, and beliefs. They run their businesses in a certain way because that is how they have always been run, and not because of analytical confirmation that the current modus operandi is still the best.

Open-mindedness creates the platform that challenges current conduct and seeks to find better solutions and strategies. The following sports example illustrates how greatness can be achieved by practicing open-mindedness and finding a new solution to an old problem.

PRACTICING OPEN-MINDEDNESS: A REVOLUTION IN THE HIGH JUMP COMPETITION

The story of U.S. high jumper Dick Fosbury has all the elements of a perfect case study to document the importance of open-mindedness in critical thinking. Fosbury was struggling to qualify for the competitive high jumping team when attending Medford High School. More specifically, he had problems using the traditional straddle technique when jumping over the bar. This technique required the athlete to move horizontally and face down over the bar.

Instead of wasting time perfecting an inefficient technique, Fosbury experimented with alternative ways to cross the bar. His early attempts at finding a better technique were ridiculed and one historian described them as "airborne seizures."[7] However, he continued his search for the optimum high jump technique. He was successful and created a back-first jumping style that allowed using running speed to catapult the jumper across the bar. In the 1968 Summer Olympics, Fosbury won the gold medal. His style of jumping, the so-called Fosbury Flop, is today the standard in high jumping around the world.

Open-mindedness is particularly important in today's world. Digitalization is disrupting the world at lightning speed. Whether or not you like digitalization is irrelevant. You must deal with it by making decisions that accurately anticipate possible future risks, disruptions, and opportunities. Sticking blindly to past traditions, rituals, and conventional wisdom has become a dangerous, possibly suicidal, strategy in today's fast-changing world.

Therefore, we need to start every day with an open mind to challenge everything around us. Are there better ways to do things? Will the future continue to reward today's business conduct and strategies or is radical change necessary? Is it reasonable to assume that current trends and developments will continue in the future? These are the type of questions critical thinkers must internalize when assessing the world around them.

STEP 3: ITEMS YOU MUST REMOVE FROM YOUR BACKPACK

Certain attitudes, tools, and concepts put your becoming a critical thinker at risk. Many of the items to be removed from your backpack are widely adopted patterns of behavior, conduct, and thinking. However, they block your success as a critical thinker and, therefore, you must part with them.

Chart 12 provides a sample list of those attitudes, concepts, and beliefs that do not support critical thinking. Look at your own conduct on a daily basis. These items have a tendency to sneak back into your backpack, even though you may have removed them earlier.

Chart 12: Things NOT to put into your backpack

THINGS THAT SHOULD NOT BE IN YOUR BACKPACK	
• (Uncritical) positive thinking • Excessive emotions • Ideologies • Impatience • Thinking-talking imbalances (too much talking, too little thinking) • Listening-talking imbalances • The use of words in superlative forms ("this is the best presentation ever") • Stress • Obsession with excessive speed	• Consensus fixation • Defensive arguments, destructive phrases, and excuses • Unproven myths • Traditions (related to thinking and decision making) • Unsubstantiated destructive phrases ("we always did it this way") • Hierarchical thinking • Greed (not to be confused with healthy ambition) • Political considerations

In my classes on critical thinking, I discuss the above list in great detail. In the context of this book, I highlight a few items.

Subscribing to ideologies is not compatible with critical thinking. Ideologists refuse to challenge their beliefs and convictions. They either overconfidently believe that challenging their ideologies is unnecessary ("everybody knows that this is the way to go") or they are afraid of evidence that could shatter the foundation of their ideologies. They are obsessed with defending their ideologies and beliefs at any price.

In the fields of social and political science, there are many ideologists. They rigorously defend their views of the world against any form of criticism. Some economists, for example, have firmly aligned themselves with particular economic theories. They proudly call themselves "Keynesians," "neo-liberals," or "monetarists." In fact, there are hundreds of ideologies to be found in the field of economics.

There is nothing wrong with fierce competition in economic ideas and theories. However, once you make your theory an ideology that you will defend against legitimate attempts of falsification and critical review, you have left the path of critical thinking. At that point, you are less concerned with examining the economic world (i.e., reality) and more focused on defending a certain, often not sufficiently proven, view of the world.

In my view, this is the reason that the discipline of economics has failed so spectacularly at anticipating major economic crises and disruptions. The Great Depression, the 1970s period of stagflation in the U.S., and the financial crisis of 2007 are only a few of many events that were missed by most economists. In the case of the 1970s stagflation period (i.e., the simultaneous occurrence of low economic growth and high inflation), most economists not only failed to anticipate this economic disruption, they disputed that stagflation was possible at all.

The same is true in politics. Most politicians and those interested in politics have aligned themselves with certain ideological views of the world and society. They defend their views vehemently instead of allowing or, even better, encouraging falsification attempts, as critical thinkers would do in their search for truth. As a result, society suffers from ideological decision making, which often creates poor conditions. Most societies live substantially below their true potential.

Stress and our obsession with speed are also well-known enemies of critical thinking. Our brains seem to be hardwired to respond to stress and danger with two generic strategies: fight or flight.[8] These two default strategies had been enormously successful through most of human history. For example, when we accidentally crossed the path of a wild animal, we did not have the time for detailed analysis. We needed to make a quick decision: fight the animal or run away.

Today's world, however, is fundamentally different from the past. Most of today's risks and opportunities do not appear within seconds or minutes. Instead, both severe risks and exceptional opportunities emerge over extended periods of time. Even in technology, the most dynamic field of human activity, there are very few disruptions that occur out of the blue and require a fight or flight response.

The internet, for example, has evolved over decades. Most disruptions caused by the internet and digitalization could have been anticipated by those practicing critical thinking. For example, the highly successful company Amazon emerged step by step over more than two decades. Its ability to succeed in disrupting one industry after another is a product of critical thinking applied to finding vulnerable business systems. Amazon's success is significantly aided by the lack of critical thinking of its competitors.

Amazon's success is not a story of breakneck speed. It is the story of a company that consistently applies critical thinking to offer better solutions to customers. The lesson learned is that stress and an obsession with speed often prevent us from conducting sufficient analysis. We hurry to make decisions and to implement actions. Not surprisingly, we either fall back to one of the default strategies (i.e., fight or flight) or we reach decisions that are derived from incomplete, false, or superficial analysis.

A high level of ambition is needed to succeed in life. However, many people mistake greed for high ambition. Greed is "an inordinate and insatiable longing for unneeded excess"[9] and thus not compatible with the critical thinking process. Greed tends to lead to typical boom-bust outcomes (financial bubbles in the stock markets typically thrive on greed). The greedy person or organization often experiences the same fate as Icarus in Greek mythology. Encouraged by his initial success at being able to fly by using artificial wings that were held together with wax, Icarus ignored his father's advice not to get too close to the sun. Eventually, the heat of the sun melted the wax that held his wings together and Icarus fell to his death. Lesson learned: High levels of ambition must have a place in your backpack, but you must know the difference between high ambition and greed.

STEP 4: BAN THESE WORDS FROM YOUR VOCABULARY

Certain words and phrases can be destructive to any critical thinking process. They should be eliminated from your vocabulary when engaging in critical thinking projects.

For example, a supervisor gives a presentation to his subordinates about the future strategy of the company. He closes with the questions: "What do you think?" "Does what I said make sense?" "Do you agree?"

Before you can even start your critical thinking process, it is likely that at least one colleague shouts: "Brilliant. Absolutely agree. Let's do it." Very likely, others soon follow with similar remarks.

At this moment, critical thinking has been sabotaged and is unlikely to occur. A dangerous momentum has been created to adopt uncritically the strategic proposal presented by the supervisor. This happens very often in companies around the world and explains why so many companies make so many poor decisions. No presentation or recommendation can be so perfect that it deserves spontaneous and unconditional approval. There are always issues that should be analyzed, discussed, and possibly revisited. Critical reflection almost always makes a proposal or strategy better.

Once some members of an organization have expressed their enthusiastic and unconditional support, it is nearly impossible to employ critical thinking. It will be hard for the same team members to backpedal and admit that some parts of the presentation need more analysis. They would lose face and therefore are likely to continue their support even if credible evidence shows the need for more analysis or serious revisions of the proposal.

The presenter will feel encouraged after receiving such strong support. As a result, the team members who raise (justified) critical questions will be seen as difficult and dysfunctional.

> Real world example:
>
> One of the most successful consulting companies in the world is well aware of the problem described above. Therefore, the firm has adopted an unusual principle: the obligation to dissent. It encourages all staff members across all hierarchies to criticize and challenge each other. This is done to identify weak reasoning and potentially faulty arguments. Dissent seen as an obligation prevents fast-track approvals that are backed only by hierarchy and not by analysis.

An easy way to avoid such deficiencies and impediments to critical thinking is to ban certain words and phrases. Chart 13 shows a selection of words and phrases that are incompatible with critical thinking. Feel free to add your own suggestions to the list. This list includes superlatives (e.g., the *best* presentation I ever heard), adjectives that suggest perfection (e.g., brilliant), and other phrases that hinder critical thinking. I have suggested to companies to enforce this rule by having a piggy bank that must be fed every time one of the banned words or phrases is used (the funds can support a local charity). This simple game helps an organization create better conditions for fostering critical thinking.

Chart 13: Words and phrases that impair critical thinking (examples)

DO NOT USE LIST	
<ul><li>Absolutely</li><li>Great</li><li>Brilliant</li><li>Definitely</li><li>Exceptionally</li><li>All forms of superlatives (e.g., best ever)</li></ul>	<ul><li>"Everybody knows that …" (when the truth of the statement has not yet been established)</li><li>"Couldn't agree more …"</li><li>Unrelated analogies</li><li>Excellent</li><li>Superb</li><li>"There is nothing to add or comment …"</li></ul>

You may encounter some difficulties when implementing this step. There is a trend in modern society to give overly, often undeserved, positive feedback. We see this trend when looking at school grades ("grade inflation"), performance evaluations at work, and casual feedback (e.g., restaurant reviews).

This is a dangerous development as not only is it dishonest, but it also promotes mediocrity. Every time you call something brilliant or great, it manifests the perception of having peaked on a performance scale. Consequently, performers who receive such feedback will not perceive the need to improve their performances. Quite likely, performance standards may be relaxed in the belief that current performance levels already exceed required standards.

This is a dangerous path for both individuals and society. The quality of products and services will deteriorate over time and mediocrity will be the new normal. Critical thinking in such situations will become an irritating activity performed by "negative" and "disagreeable" people.

> **Anecdote: Why great teachers refuse to give great grades**
>
> When I attended high school in Germany, I came across two great teachers. They not only were competent and dedicated as were many of my other teachers, they also added enormous value to their students' portfolios of relevant skills. They did so by simply restricting the use of words that would signal perfection and greatness. There was no inflated use of the words "great" or "brilliant" to describe our work. Also, at the beginning of the school year, we were told that it was unlikely that anyone in the class would be awarded a straight "A" grade. In fact, their grades were typically a whole grade lower than those given by other teachers for similar performance standards.
>
> The result was that students employed a lot of critical thinking when drafting papers and homework. We constantly critiqued our own work to search relentlessly for improvement opportunities and inconsistencies, knowing that any weakness certainly would have been detected and critiqued by our teacher. Needless to say, the learning success with

> these two teachers was phenomenal, even though it meant much more work for the students.

There is a third group of responses that should be banned in critical thinking projects, unrelated analogies. Unrelated analogies are frequently used to trap an unsuspecting audience. Master class manipulators use them to make an unproven claim or hypothesis look like a true statement. I have seen many rhetorically skilled people use this tool successfully to manipulate the decision making of their audiences.

For example, I met a person who is a true champion in using unrelated analogies. If he wanted a group of business managers to vote for a certain strategic option, he would simply relate the option to an analogy that could not be disputed. The only problem was that this analogy in reality had nothing to do with the strategic option being discussed. The example: "Following your old strategy is like hoping your car continues to run after the engine has been removed."

Politicians are masters in using unrelated analogies. The fact that they get away with it says much about the state of critical thinking in modern society. Pay close attention to this the next time you listen to a political debate.

STEP 5: BUILD A NETWORK OF PEOPLE WHO CHALLENGE YOUR VIEWS

If you studied psychology or sociology, you may have come across a concept known as "confirmation bias." It basically states that we actively look for information that confirms our views and beliefs. For example, most investors are likely to look for articles and research that confirm their original views about investments, not those that present opposite views. Supporters of a political party tend to prefer newspapers and television channels that are known for sharing the same political view. At cocktail parties and other social events, we tend to spend time with people who share our views on life, politics, and other topics. We also choose to socialize with people who are similar to us. Typically, we went to the same school, work in the same industry, or have similar geographic roots.

From a critical thinking perspective, confirmation bias and related behavior lead to terrible outcomes. We voluntarily eliminate a rich source of new and possibly valuable information from our analysis. As a result, we base consequential decisions on shaky foundations. Even worse, filtered and biased information reinforces unjustified views and beliefs. This is a problem not only for an individual. It is also a major problem for society, as it may lead to continued poor decision making and unpreparedness for new challenges.

During the period of the so-called "New Economy" (late 1990s to early 2000s), many people formed the belief that internet stocks were highly attractive investments that would continue to outperform the general market for the foreseeable future.

There were several experts who expressed doubts about this view of the world. I was one of them. As a risk management consultant, I offered several arguments that the hype about internet stocks not only was exaggerated, but also based on faulty analytical foundations.

In my presentations, I provided an analogy for the internet hype in business history that ended in a great disaster. During the 1920s, new technologies such as the radio initiated an economic boom and people were enthusiastic about a "new economic era" (note the similarity to the term "new economy"). Politicians, such as U.S. President Calvin Coolidge, jumped on the "growth forever" bandwagon. He described the U.S. in a State of the Union Address in late 1928 as being in *"an era of prosperity"* and that Americans should *"anticipate the future with optimism."*[10] His successor, President Herbert Hoover, described the U.S. situation in 1929 as follows: *"We in America today are nearer to the final triumph over poverty than ever before in the history of any land."*[11] As we all know, these enthusiastic optimistic remarks were made months before one of the most severe economic crises occurred: the Great Depression. What followed was a stock market crash, high unemployment rates, a severe, long-lasting economic depression, and great misery for almost everyone.

This example demonstrates one of the most colossal failures in economic and financial history. It was a mixture of superficial thinking, greed, and herd mentality that enabled such an epic economic crisis and extreme level of collective unpreparedness. Back in the early 2000s and late 2006, periods of peak optimism followed by major financial crises, it was not very different in terms of superficial thinking, greed, and herd mentality. Several reputable experts and companies warned about the fragility of the new economic bubble. But those warnings of an impending crisis either were ignored or ridiculed. The key mistake was that decision makers failed to surround themselves with dissenting thinkers. Hence, their faulty analyses and poor decisions remained unchallenged until it was too late to correct course.

We should learn from such failures by surrounding ourselves with people who do not share our views and have different backgrounds, skills, thinking patterns, and experiences. These people are invaluable as they will point out inconsistencies and errors in our thinking. They provide free stress testing and valuable learning experiences. They also widen our horizons, which may help us to anticipate future risks and opportunities. A diverse network of individuals will likely become one of your most decisive competitive advantages. Chart 14 suggests some methods for accomplishing this.

Chart 14: Diversifying your social network and gaining valuable new insights

ACTIVITIES TO DIVERSIFY YOUR SOCIAL NETWORK
• Make a list of skills, experiences, and backgrounds that are missing in your social network. Attend events where you are likely to meet people who can fill these gaps. • Seek out people who share different views about important topics (e.g., investment markets). Write down their counterarguments and evaluate them critically. Try to become friends with these people. • At social gatherings, try to find people who do not share your view of the world or who have distinctively different backgrounds.

For example, if you are heavily invested in the stock market (i.e., you have a positive view of stocks), you would be naïve not to seek out those who disagree with your view. They will help you stress test your hypotheses about continuing appreciation of stock prices. People who disagree with your hypotheses are likely to find faults or inconsistencies in your analyses that back your hypotheses and conviction (if there are any). The benefit is that they are good at it (as they uphold different views and hypotheses) and they stress test your reasoning for free.

Once you have started diversifying your social network, you should do the same with your media selections. Read articles and watch programs that are known for their diverse backgrounds and perspectives. You must make sure that you have access to all relevant information when making consequential decisions. A good way to accomplish this is by including foreign media outlets in your source of information. Many of them provide English translations of their content or are even conducted in English. Limiting your information intake to the sources that agree with your views is a serious shortcoming, particularly in an era of globalization.

Summary:

In this chapter, the following tools, frameworks, and concepts are discussed:

- The *five initial steps to becoming a critical thinker*
- *Constructive skepticism*
- *Effective Slowness*
- Backpack content for your journey to becoming a critical thinker (what to bring, what not to bring)
- Words to ban from your vocabulary (*do not use list* of words that impair critical thinking)
- How to diversify your social network
- How to diversify the sources of your information intake

Exercises:

Conduct the following exercises linked to the five-step program for becoming a critical thinker (as outlined in the previous chapter):

Step 1: Conduct the exercise described in the text (regarding *constructive skepticism*).

Step 2: Compare the model backpack described in the text with the backpack you used in the past when making consequential decisions (e.g., career move, material investment decisions). What are the differences? Would the model backpack have led to better life outcomes?

Step 3: Apply the exercise for step 2 to step 3. When making material decisions in the past, which of the *do not bring items* made it into your backpack? How did they impact your decision making and life outcomes?

Step 4: During a business meeting, mentally count how often those banned words are used. Try to detect certain patterns. For example, how often do highly successful people (e.g., top managers with long-term successful track records) use such banned words? Watch interviews on television with highly accomplished people (e.g., long-term successful sport coaches, investors, top managers) and conduct this exercise. Note the number of times people misuse banned words (e.g., superlatives) to describe a performance standard that was, at best, good or average.

Step 5: At your next social event, try to spend time with at least three people who are distinctively different from you in terms of background, education, interests, or political opinions. Ask them their views on a material topic such as health, managing finances and investments, or professional career planning. Did they add value to your decision making? If so, how?

CHAPTER 3 -THE ORANGE BELT: THE FOUR PRAGMATIC NAVIGATION POINTS FOR CRITICAL THINKING

The field of critical thinking with all its different approaches, concepts, and tools can be overwhelming for beginners. Therefore, I have developed a navigation framework that might help you get started and stay on course for becoming a black belt critical thinker (after you have completed the introductory five-step program described in the previous chapter). I call this framework "The Four Pragmatic Navigation Points for Critical Thinking." You can use this framework the same way a sailor uses a lighthouse at night to navigate through dangerous reefs and waters.

Let me stress again that critical thinking is an approach that can be employed in all aspects of life, including professional career management, personal growth, health improvement, and all social activities. In this chapter, I use examples from sports, health care, and financial management. I focus on one case in particular: the German national soccer team as it went from being the laughingstock of international soccer in 2004 to world champion in 2014.[12] This transformation was very much a product of applying tools and concepts of critical thinking to a real world performance problem. This case study is an insightful example that demonstrates the power of critical thinking.

> **A side note on the German national soccer team:** During the 2018 World Cup in Russia, the team performed disastrously as it was eliminated in the early group stage of the tournament. In my view, past successes made the team complacent, lazy, and overconfident. We see such patterns quite often in success research. In fact, in soccer there is the curse of the World Cup winner, as France (2002), Italy (2010), and Spain (2014), after winning the previous World Cup, were eliminated at the initial group stage of the next tournament. Winning often leads to arrogance, exaggerated self-confidence, superficial thinking, and political debates and clashes. None of these is compatible with critical

> thinking, but part of the "winner's curse." We are reminded of the constant struggle to defend and extend past success.

We return to the framework of "The Four Pragmatic Navigation Points for Critical Thinking," which is shown in chart 15. Each navigation point is discussed in the following paragraphs.

Chart 15: The Four Pragmatic Navigation Points of Critical Thinking

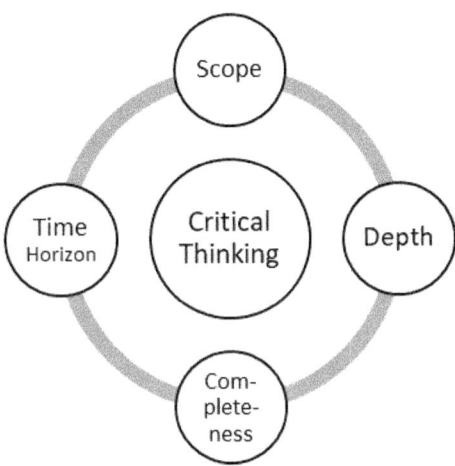

Please keep in mind that successful conduct requires sufficient attention given to all four navigation points. For example, in chart 16, different approaches of critical thinking are mapped against the four navigation points of critical thinking.

Case 1 shows a solid analysis that satisfies the requirements of all four navigation points (scores for all four navigation points come close to one hundred percent). Case 2 is a "quick and dirty" approach that is likely to lead to suboptimal decisions and subsequently to poor outcomes (low scores for all navigation points). The attention given to the four navigation points is not sufficient. Case 3 is an example of good analysis except for its overly short-term focus (low score for time horizon). This is a common problem today. Politicians and business leaders often ignore long-term implications of their decisions, simply because their incentive structures do not reward long-term thinking and decision making.

Chart 16: *The Four Pragmatic Navigation Points* – different approaches (illustrative)

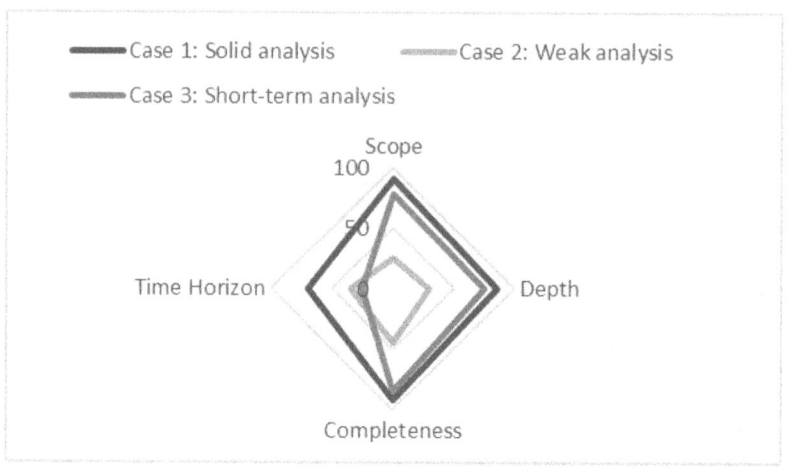

Let us discuss the navigation points in detail.

NAVIGATION POINT ONE: SCOPE OF OUR ANALYSIS AND THINKING

The first navigation point is concerned with the scope of the analyses used in critical thinking activities. Obviously, an analysis that is too narrowly defined may miss crucial insights and lead to poor decisions. However, a too widely defined scope of analysis may distract from the real issues at hand. Both cases are likely to lead to suboptimal decisions and are unacceptable.

A too narrow scope of analysis is often the result of

- (perceived) time pressure
- limited resources
- laziness
- distraction
- a lack of open-mindedness for new solutions and innovations.

Such issues may stand in the way of our gaining a thorough understanding of an issue and prevent us from arriving at good decisions and valuable solutions.

A good example of a too narrow scope of analysis is the so-called nine dot problem illustrated in chart 17. The task is to connect nine dots with four straight lines without taking your pencil off the paper. The problem can be solved only when widening the scope of analysis beyond the area marked by the nine dots.[13]

Chart 17: Setting the *Scope* for Critical Thinking: The *Nine Dot Problem*

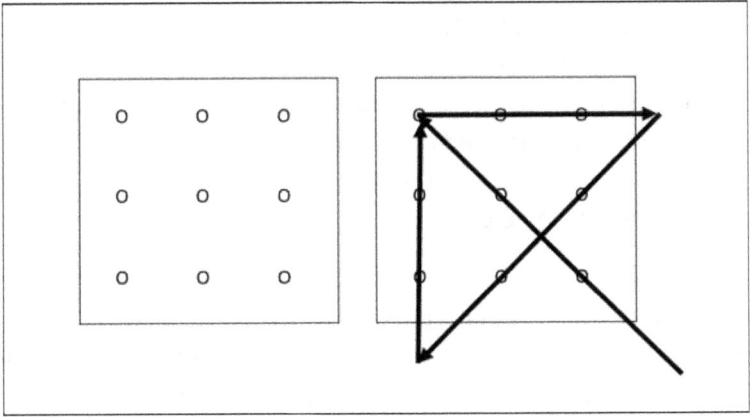

In the corporate world, we find many examples where executives and teams struggle to set the right scope for their analyses. Often, their analyses are too narrowly defined and therefore important issues are missed. We find this problem often in the context of risk management activities in the financial world.

For example, prior to the financial crisis of 2007, risk management analyses of most financial institutions assumed that future outcomes in financial markets were more or less a continuous linear trend with no severe disruptions. Consequently, many important risk issues were either neglected or were dismissed too early as irrelevant or highly unlikely. As a result, financial institutions failed to prepare for the following risk scenarios (examples):

1. U.S. house prices fall nationwide
2. A high number of mortgage holders default on their debt
3. Short-term funding markets for financial liquidity shut down and become unavailable for an extended period
4. Major financial institutions fail to meet their obligations or suffer major credit losses leading to contagious instability.

It did not require rocket science to come up with these four basic risk scenarios. In fact, some risk management experts warned of these long before 2007, but financial institutions ignored these warnings and continued to conduct narrowly defined risk management analyses. The commonly shared but unchallenged assumption was that conditions would continue on the present trajectory.

The example demonstrates the importance of setting the right scope for analysis. In very competitive situations, such as sports, it can be advantageous to choose a much wider scope to find new sources for competitive advantages and strategic development. You may leapfrog past your competitors making it difficult for them to catch up.

The following example explains this important point. It is taken from a case study about the dramatic fall and subsequent rise of the German national soccer team between 2004 and 2014:[14]

In 2004, German soccer was in a pitiful state. Following a disastrous performance at the European Championship in Belgium and the Netherlands, there was no optimism and no hope. Young talent seemed to be plentiful in other countries, but not in Germany. Two years before the World Cup being played in Germany, a continued slide of German soccer's competitiveness seemed inevitable.

At that time, the German soccer association hired Juergen Klinsmann as manager. What followed is in my view one of the most successful critical thinking projects that led to radical structural reforms. Klinsmann, with assistant coach Joachim Loew and sports director Oliver Bierhoff, started an analytic process of searching for new sources of competitive advantages. They set the analytic scope of their critical thinking process extremely wide. Everything was questioned, radical critical thinking encouraged, and experiences from other sports disciplines and science welcomed. Two concrete examples demonstrate this. First, the team quickly realized that player fitness was a key issue. They hired U.S. fitness coaches who introduced position-specific fitness programs to the German squad. Initially, the players were skeptical about the new awkward routines and the new fitness coaches,[15] but with the first results, the players readily welcomed them. Second, the coaching team looked at a wide array of new ideas to make the team more successful in specific aspects of the game. Anecdotal evidence suggests that coaches and stars from other sports disciplines (e.g., American football, field hockey, Formula One car racing) were interviewed to gain new ideas. Also, the coaching team consulted with psychologists, sports science experts, data analysts, watch makers, and other professionals to gain new ideas about creating new forms of competitive advantage.

This is a wonderful example for creating sustainable competitive advantages by increasing the scope of analysis. The German soccer coaches found performance drivers and levers that most other teams neglected or ignored.

There is one caveat. Widening the scope of analysis is not an end in itself. In some situations, the real causes of a problem may become clear at an early stage of the analytic process. In such cases it does not make sense to maintain a wide analytic scope. Scope should be limited, while the depth of analysis, as explained in the following paragraphs, should increase.

Experience is needed to set an appropriate scope for any critical thinking process. For the inexperienced critical thinker, it may be advisable to choose a wider scope for analytic work that is required for making important decisions.

NAVIGATION POINT TWO: DEPTH OF ANALYSIS AND THINKING

To be successful, critical thinking and required analyses must be pushed to an appropriate depth. Superficial analysis is not an acceptable option as it typically leads to suboptimal decisions. Unfortunately, the depth of analyses today is decreasing at an alarming rate.

Resource constraints often prevent us from pressing the analysis to deeper levels. In such cases, it is legitimate to make (temporary) prioritizations. However, it is important to document those choices. Proper documentation enables us to go back to issues that were initially excluded. We do not want to miss an important insight that could dramatically improve our decision making.

Choosing the correct scope and depth of a critical thinking process is key to success. In general, there is a higher chance of success if both scope and depth are increased. A wider field provides new insights and new sources of unexploited opportunities and decisive competitive advantages. More time and resources are spent, but the costs may be dramatically outweighed by emerging opportunities. Chart 18 illustrates this important point.

Assume that the scope/depth profiles shown in chart 18 are those of two competing soccer teams: the grey and the black. Both teams have performed unsuccessfully in the past and try to use critical thinking to reverse their fortunes.

Chart 18: Two competing choices of *Scope/Depth* combinations (grey team versus black team)

	SCOPE OF A CRITICAL THINKING PROCESS/ANALYSIS List of factors influencing competitive outcomes													
	Factor A	Factor B	Factor C	Factor D	Factor E	Factor F	Factor G	Factor H	Factor I	Factor J	Factor K	Factor L	Factor M	Factor N
1														
2														
3														
4														
5														
6														
7														
8														
9														
10														

(DEPTH OF ANALYSIS)

Looking at the scope/depth profile of the analyses conducted by both soccer teams, the grey team is likely to do better than the black team. The black team's strategic analysis is very limited in both scope and depth. We can assume that the black team will more or less continue to do what it did in the past.

The grey team widened the scope of analysis and looked at additional factors that could lead to better strategies and tactics (e.g. psychological studies on motivation, team cohesiveness, and focus). The grey team's analyses were conducted in great depth, giving an additional advantage over the black team.

Looking at the German national soccer team gives us a real-world case study on this topic. Judging from media reports, the scope and depth of analysis that the German team used since 2004 is likely to set a new standard in soccer strategy. The managers of the German soccer team left no stone unturned to find new sources of competitive advantage.

An example from the 2014 World Cup illustrates this point. The German coaches paid close attention to creating strong team spirit and cohesiveness. This is not a trivial challenge. Most team members played for competing club teams during the regular season (e.g., Bayern Munich, Dortmund, Arsenal London, Real Madrid). Additionally, some players came from clubs that historically had intense rivalry (e.g., Munich, Dortmund, Schalke). To ensure the best possible team cohesiveness, the German team had chosen a new lodging concept. Instead of following the traditional path of renting a hotel with single or double rooms, the German team chose a new approach. They occupied a tourist resort that consisted of several bungalows that groups of four to six players shared. In fact, the tourist resort was newly built and completed for the World Cup.[16] The resort had several additional advantages. It was located in the same climate zone as the group stage games of the German team (Note: Brazil consists of different climate zones). It was close to an airport, but away from a big city (limiting exposure to distractions and noise).

Groups of players were assigned to each cottage. Those players were not on the same club teams. Anecdotal evidence suggests that this innovative lodging concept was a key factor in creating strong team spirit and a high level of team cohesiveness. I am not aware of any other team using lodging to create such team cohesiveness. Experts credited the success of the German team at the 2014 World Cup mostly to its convincing team spirit and discipline.[17] While other teams relied on famous mega-stars such as Messi and Ronaldo, Germany relied on its cohesive team.

It is important to note that widening the scope of analysis alone will not dramatically improve the outcome of a critical thinking project. It is the combination of expanded scope and increased depth of analysis that makes the difference. In this context, the German national soccer team is a great case study. They analyzed in great depth a wide range of factors that could directly or indirectly influence the outcome of a soccer game. They found new sources of competitive advantages unknown to their competition.

NAVIGATION POINT THREE: TIME HORIZON

One common mistake in critical thinking projects is to focus on short-term outcomes that may provide some benefits, but hurt us tremendously in the long term.

For example, we may save some money by buying lower grade products for a house renovation, but in the long term the costs of repairs and the inconvenience will clearly outweigh the initial savings. In the corporate world, strategic decisions often boost short-term revenues, but ignore the costs of future risks or issues excluded from analysis.

The financial crisis of 2007 is a good example of this issue. The strategy of repackaging debt (i.e., originating loans and mortgages and bundling them as investment products) and trading it was an attractive strategy for banks to increase profitability in the short term. It led to substantial appreciation of banks' share prices. However, banks failed to understand the long-term implications of this strategy. While short-term profits soared, banks' balance sheets accumulated substantial risk exposures.[18] These risk exposures then turned into massive losses. In many cases, later stage losses (and fines for misconduct) exceeded the original profits.

Therefore, any critical thinking activity must ensure that the time horizon of the analysis includes both short- and long-term considerations. Any initiative or decision must be analyzed for several iterations of possible consequences. Each action leads to new consequences and new outcomes that can be positive or negative.

It is advisable to target between four and five iterations of potential consequences of a decision. The critical thinking team should ask the question "and then, what happens?" at least four times to make sure that long-term consequences of a contemplated strategy are fully understood. Had top managers of financial institutions done this simple exercise, the financial crisis of 2007 would not have reached such dramatic proportions.

To facilitate this important task, I developed a concept called the *Law of the 4.5^{th} Consequence*, the optimal number of *"and then, what will happen?"* iterations. Fewer than four iterations risks missing important long-term consequences. More than five iterations, however, often create unmanageable complexity and limited value creation. Therefore, in many cases focusing on four to five iterations is initially sufficient. The number of iterations needs to be related to your situation. In more complex cases, computers are required to simulate vastly larger numbers of iterations. It may be advisable to use logic trees when applying the *Law of the 4.5^{th} Consequence*. This is particularly helpful when an iteration of *"and then, what will happen?"* produces more than one possible outcome.

In my view, decision makers in politics and business often limit themselves to a maximum of two or three iterations. Consequently, their decisions often backfire in the long term.

Putting the *Law of the 4.5^{th} Consequence* into action is relatively simple. Chart 19 shows a simple framework to get started (again, please feel free to use logic trees to summarize more complex outcomes). The most important point is to force (!) yourself to think diligently of the long-term consequences of material decisions you are about to make. [19]

Chart 19: Illustrative practice sheet for the *Law of the 4.5th Consequence*

THE *LAW OF THE 4.5th CONSEQUENCE*
What will happen if I make the following material decision:
(Describe the decision) _____
1. Consequence: _____
2. Consequence: _____
3. Consequence: _____
4. Consequence: _____
5. Consequence: _____

Both positive and negative consequences should be included. The first two or three consequences of a material decision may lead to neutral or positive outcomes. The analysis should continue as substantial changes may occur at the fourth or fifth consequence.

A case example is presented in chart 20. Assume a soccer team considers changing its game philosophy by moving from a defensive strategy (i.e., strong defense and slow play) to a fast-paced attacking and pressing style, which has become the strategy of many top teams. The German team did this when Klinsmann became head coach in 2004.

Such a serious move threatens success in the long term. The risks appear at the end of the season, the decisive period (i.e. during play-offs, UEFA Champions League semi-finals and final). In chart 20, such a strategic shift is shown to backfire and create issues just when the adopted strategy is irreversible. The example illustrates the later stage problems that occurred after the coach changed the strategy of play.

The lesson is to avoid being blindsided by early success. Important decisions and new strategies require detailed thought. Such analysis must include the *Law of the 4.5th Consequence* or similar approaches to understand later stage consequences of a decision.

Chart 20: The *Law of the 4.5th Consequence* in Practice – a soccer team

The following decision was made: *Moving from a slow, defensive to a fast attacking, pressing style of play. Targeted implementation date: start of new season.* Here is what happened:	
Consequence 1 (summer break)	• Summer is used to practice the new game strategy; everyone excited
Consequence 2 (first month)	• The new strategy surprises opposing teams; many games won • Fans love it; great reviews from media
Consequence 3 (following months)	• New playing style is physically extremely demanding on players; key players show signs of exhaustion • Team loses games during the last 15 minutes due to exhaustion (lack of qualified substitutes becomes a problem)
Consequence 4 (later stage season)	• Key players have trouble keeping up with the physical demands (more running, more sprints); more injuries
Consequence 5 (last month of season)	• Several key players injured miss the end of the season; many matches lost; after a great start, team fails to achieve its goals

Several soccer teams fell into this trap by ignoring the long-term consequences of a chosen soccer strategy. There are several countermeasures a coach could have initiated to avoid these pitfalls. For example, having more qualified players would have allowed more rest periods for key players (assuming financial resources allowed such a move). These coaches failed to understand that they did not have the quality and quantity of players for this particular strategy.

When the German national team switched to a more attacking style, they dealt with the long-term consequences. They allowed two years to make the switch for the 2006 World Cup. New players had the physicality for this new strategy. As a consequence, many established players lost out to younger players who were fitter and faster. Team management observed the progress of players' fitness (e.g., regular fitness tests). After a disastrous campaign at the Euro 2004, the German team astonished fans by finishing third in the 2006 World Cup playing an attractive attacking style of soccer.

The *Law of the 4.5th Consequence* can analyze long-term consequences of many different decisions. For example, when discussing successful career strategies with students, I suggest the application of this concept to study fourth and fifth order consequences of certain career strategies.

NAVIGATION POINT FOUR: COMPLETENESS OF ANALYSIS AND THINKING

The last navigation point for successful critical thinking projects is a thorough check for completeness of analyses.

Often, analysis is incomplete. For example, there is discussion in the U.S. on how to reform health care. Many insurance models and their financial implications are considered. The analysis, however, is incomplete and therefore is unlikely to lead to satisfying outcomes. A classic violation of the fourth navigation point of critical thinking is the reason for this failure.

Current analysis of the U.S. health care system takes illness as a given. Lifestyle changes (e.g., better nutrition, more activity, preventive health actions) could reduce the amount of illness requiring expensive medical care. Many diseases that lead to fast rising health care costs are often self-inflicted by poor lifestyle choices and ignorance (e.g., type 2 diabetes, cardiovascular diseases, obesity). In many cases, poor health can be reversed or at least improved by making better lifestyle choices.[20] Decision makers fail to include these important issues in their analyses.

In addition, past analyses did not include consideration of successful programs in other countries. For example, most medical procedures and drugs cost significantly less in Germany (normally a high cost country) and other European countries than in the U.S. Decision makers should learn from other countries by analyzing such alternative approaches.

The U.S. health care system offers expensive treatment after patients become seriously ill. Employing critical thinking and thorough analyses could solve the current health care dilemma in the U.S.

To ensure completeness of your analyses, chart 21 lists a selection of questions to test your analytic rigor. This is a starting point; add your own questions for a basic checklist of your analytic work.

Chart 21: Sample checklist for completeness of critical thinking activities

COMPLETENESS OF CRITICAL THINKING – SAMPLE CHECKLIST
• Have all relevant factors and levers for the desired outcome been identified and analyzed? • Has research from experts offering contradictory views and hypotheses been included? • Have all relevant best and worst case examples been identified and evaluated? What are the lessons learned? • Have cross dependencies among different factors/issues been identified and analyzed? • Have all available experts and qualified people been interviewed to improve the critical thinking process? • Have all relevant and available data sources improved the analysis and the critical thinking process? • Have all relevant and available research projects been included? • Has sufficient time been allowed to perform all required analytical tasks?

- Have all conclusions been sufficiently stress-tested by counter-examples or by an expert playing devil's advocate?
- Have all recommendations and decisions been tested for their short- and long-term consequences?

If all these questions have been addressed, your analytic work and decisions seem to be in good shape.

Using the four navigation points is a simple procedure that can improve the outcome of any critical thinking project. Appropriate choices of scope, depth, time horizon, and completeness of your analytic work are key factors for long-term success. When you are experienced in critical thinking, the four navigation points will be set easily. Until then, it may help to use the frameworks and suggestions presented in this chapter.

Congratulations, after reading this text and doing the exercises, you have passed the requirements for your orange belt. We move on to an important determinant of future success: your preparedness for mastering future challenges, risks, and opportunities. Long-term success is impossible without superb preparedness for life's volatilities. That is the key differentiator between long-term winners and losers. The winners take risks, but they are prepared to take these risks. Losers either take no risks or, even worse, they take risks for which they are not sufficiently prepared. Therefore, critical thinking should always be used to improve your general preparedness for life's volatilities and uncertainties.

Summary:

In this chapter, the following tools, frameworks, and concepts are discussed:

- The *Four Pragmatic Navigation Points of Critical Thinking* (Scope, Depth, Completeness, Time Horizon)
- *Scope-Depth Matrix* of Critical Thinking
- *Law of the 4.5th Consequence*

Exercises:

Select a project, event, or life episode that was not successful. For example, a lost client pitch, a failed attempt at a promotion at work, or an unsatisfying outcome of a major project in your personal life (e.g., building or renovating a house). Analyze how critical thinking could have been used to achieve a better outcome. Review your past analyses for the unsuccessful project by using the four navigation points for critical thinking. How well did you or your team do with each navigation point?

CHAPTER 4 - THE GREEN BELT: LEVERAGE CRITICAL THINKING TO ACHIEVE A STATE OF TOTAL STRATEGIC PREPAREDNESS

Long-term success is critically dependent on one crucial factor: a high level of preparedness for future risks and opportunities. Preparedness in this context means a positive readiness to deal successfully with a wide variety of future scenarios including risks, disruptions, structural breaks, and emerging opportunities.

Long-term success rarely occurs in the absence of good preparedness. Therefore, long-term winners are typically masters of preparedness. Preparedness is one of their highest priorities in life. Consequently, long term winners get rarely caught unprepared by an adverse development in life. Critical thinking plays a central role in achieving high levels of preparedness.

Losers typically lack preparedness. Although they may enjoy short periods of success, unpreparedness will eventually catch up with them, leading to disruptive setbacks and failures.

Long-term winners use their superior preparedness to extend the lead over their less prepared competitors. This enables them to turn risks into opportunities. Therefore, winning is typically a story of good preparedness and losing one of poor preparedness.

Preparedness is the result of applying critical thinking to an uncertain future. By asking what could happen in terms of risks, disruptions, challenges, and opportunities, we are taking the first step to reducing negative surprises. Developing proactive strategies and contingency plans is the next step to turn preparedness into competitive advantages and better outcomes, both of which rely on applying critical thinking skills to real world challenges.

Unfortunately, most people fail to do this and lessen their chances of fully exploiting their potential and enjoying long-term success. We can prepare for an uncertain future, but we need to do it the right way. Most people make a fatal mistake when analyzing future risks and opportunities. They try to predict the exact path the future will take (often referred to as a base case scenario) and then dedicate all of their preparatory work to this one scenario. Those base case scenarios are often nothing more than linear extrapolations of the recent past. Little critical thinking is used to derive these predictions. When the future takes a different path than anticipated in single case predictions, setbacks and severe losses are suffered.

Long-term successful people choose a different approach to deal with future volatility. They know that it is impossible to predict the exact path the future will take and that there will be deviations from the past. Their main focus is to understand the complete spectrum of possible future outcomes and developments. This spectrum ranges from worst case to best case scenarios. The areas of vulnerability are identified and preparedness raised.

For example, nothing is more ridiculous than the annual media ritual of asking so-called stock market experts for their year-end predictions of stock market indices. Typically, such predictions are useless as there are too many unpredictable variables that influence the stock market. In other words, the likelihood that a single point prediction will be incorrect is close to one hundred percent. We should be more concerned with the range of possible outcomes than an unreliable single point prediction. Understanding the spectrum of possible scenarios helps us to assess the overall risk of investing. This enables us to develop more appropriate investment and hedging strategies.

Unfortunately, modern life is increasingly a story of widespread unpreparedness. Our strategies for dealing with future volatility are often based on assuming that the future is a continuation of recent trends with only marginal variations. Hence, **most of us operate in an environment of dangerous unpreparedness, a bad foundation for long-term success.**

Preparedness is not a new concept; it is a forgotten one that is central to many passages of the Bible.[21] In the past, preparedness was a key life principle that guided all material decision making. It is paradoxical that today, when preparedness is needed more than ever, we are much less concerned about it. For example, the majority of financial institutions failed to prepare for stagnating or falling U.S. house prices prior to the financial crisis of 2007. Their preparedness was focused on a base case scenario that predicted that the unprecedented rise in house prices would continue for the foreseeable future. This misjudgment was remarkable in the absence of relevant demographic changes that would justify higher real estate prices.

Preparedness precedes long-term success. Preparedness is a prerequisite to achieving success. Preparedness is more than a risk avoidance strategy. It is the foundation of proactive strategies that generate decisive competitive advantages. It turns disruptions and crises into launch pads for successful conduct. Preparedness allows us to pursue opportunities that would be too risky otherwise. For example, superb preparedness enables mountain climbers to pursue challenging mountain tops without exposing themselves to unacceptable levels of risks.

To help clients achieve the levels of preparedness needed to become long-term winners, I developed a concept called "Total Strategic Preparedness." The goal is to turn preparedness into a powerful success enabler. *Total Strategic Preparedness* is an advanced application of critical thinking to fulfill the requirements of the three levels of preparedness:

1. ***Defensive preparedness***, which protects against major risk events.
2. ***Proactive preparedness***, which seeks to leverage our defensive preparedness into strategies that create competitive advantages.
3. ***Disruptive preparedness***, which seeks to create disruptions and events that will catch others (competitors) by surprise, giving us a decisive advantage.

Before we discuss the concept *of Total Strategic Preparedness* in more detail, we need to familiarize ourselves with the factors that are responsible for today's crisis of widespread unpreparedness. Understanding these factors is the basis for putting *Total Strategic Preparedness* into action.

MODERN SOCIETY FACES A CRISIS OF UNPREPAREDNESS

Modern society is far removed from the requirements of *Total Strategic Preparedness*. Our lack of critical thinking has put us in a state of dangerous unpreparedness. There are many threats for which society is poorly prepared in political, economic, financial, and social areas.

In most cases unpreparedness is self-inflicted, rooted in either negligence or stubborn unwillingness to use critical thinking. Disruptions and risks can be anticipated and, at least partly, mitigated. Severe risk events rarely occur out of the blue. In most cases, credible experts had issued warnings long before a severe risk event occurred (see chart 22).

Chart 22: Catastrophic risks are rarely unpredictable (examples)

Risk Event	Public warnings by credible experts?
Great Depression of 1929	Yes
World War I/World War II	Yes
Collapse of the internet bubble, 2002	Yes
Banking crisis, 2007-2008	Yes
Collapse of the U.S. residential real estate market, 2007-2009	Yes
Nuclear catastrophe at Fukushima, Japan, 2011	Yes
Ebola cases emerge in developed world, 2014	Yes
Hurricane Andrew in Florida, 1992	Yes

There are at least seven powerful forces that explain society's failure to achieve sufficient levels of preparedness:[22]

1. Laziness, complacency, and distractions
2. Arrogance and overconfidence
3. Incomplete, superficial, or faulty analyses
4. Obsession with short-term success
5. Manipulation by others (e.g., media, leaders, majority views)
6. Positive thinking leading to unrealistic view of future risks and opportunities
7. Living in a sixty percent world

The seventh force, living in a sixty percent world, alludes to a much bigger problem. The new normal standard of performance seems to be at about sixty percent of our true potential. This is true for professional activities, products manufactured, services performed, and many other activities. We are too distracted, unmotivated, complacent, and unprepared to exploit our full potential. Our aspiration level seems to be capped at a sixty percent level of our true potential. This includes all analytical work that precedes decision making.

This explains why many products and services fail to achieve the longevity and reliability of those of a generation ago. For example, my parents' generation expected a refrigerator to operate faultlessly for at least twenty years or more. They would never have bought an extended warranty policy covering years two to five because early failure was extremely rare. If it did happen, most companies would have been so disconcerted by the poor quality they delivered to the customer that they would have repaired the product for free. Today, manufacturing products at a sixty percent quality level has become a profitable endeavor for many companies. They earn additional money from repairs, costly maintenance, expensive extended warranty insurance contracts, and earlier replacement purchases. This comes at an enormous cost due to mountains of waste (often containing hazardous materials) and a misallocation of resources. For consumers, the sixty percent world presents increased financial pressure.[23]

Today, in the sixty percent aspiration world, a new refrigerator (or any appliance or consumer electronics product) with ten years of faultless operation is rare. While there are many new innovations, gimmicks, and extended functionality a product offers (e.g., some refrigerators come with touchscreens and smartphone connections), there is little (if any) improvement in quality, longevity, and reliability. We operate under a quality aspiration of "just high enough not to get into trouble." The result is a sixty percent standard of performance.

A sixty percent standard is a poor starting point for achieving good levels of preparedness for future volatility and uncertainty. Future setbacks caused by unpreparedness are almost a certainty. It is alarming that we find sixty percent preparedness levels almost everywhere including in politics, business, education, and risk management. This issue will haunt us in the future. In many aspects of modern life, we operate at dangerous levels of collective unpreparedness for adverse developments.

We need to employ critical thinking to avoid these seven forces of unpreparedness. We need to leave the sixty percent world, particularly when it concerns our analytical work. The following provides some suggestions on how to accomplish this.

HOW PREPAREDNESS WORKS

Getting caught unprepared by a risk event sets us up for failure, reducing our chances for long-term success. Being caught unprepared exposes us to the following threats:

- **Time pressure**: There is not enough time to conduct comprehensive and diligent analysis required for good decision making. We are forced to rush into important decisions.
- **Fight-or-flight response:**[24] This is a physiological reaction to a stressful event (e.g., our material unpreparedness). The human decision-making system is programmed to reduce responses to any stressful event to two options: fight or flight. While the reduction of possible responses to two options worked well in the

past (e.g., encountering a wild animal), they are clearly suboptimal in modern society. A third option is needed: rational analysis to arrive at a logically sound decision. However, this option is not part of our "biological operating system" and it requires time for critical thinking. Most people, even many top managers, respond to situations of stressful unpreparedness with simple and insufficient fight-or-flight strategies.[25]

- **Panic/emotional instability**: People operating under stressful conditions caused by unpreparedness panic and become emotionally unstable. This makes them vulnerable to poor decision making and irrational behavior.
- **Following unqualified leaders**: Unpreparedness causes us to seek help from other people. There is a danger that we turn to unqualified, charismatic leaders or dangerous demagogues. We are also likely to succumb to groupthink or populism.

To avoid such a downward spiral in decision making and performance, it is important to have a high level of preparedness regardless of what the future brings. We need to anticipate possible risks and challenges and avoid surprises. Surprises are typically evidence of unpreparedness. To do so, I developed a concept, *Strategic Future Anticipation*. It provides the intelligence and insight needed to derive effective preparedness strategies. *Strategic Future Anticipation* creates a radar screen that includes all relevant risks and opportunities that could emerge in the future. By using scenario analyses, expert interviews, and other techniques, we construct a comprehensive compilation of future situations and outcomes that require preparatory actions. The goal is to eliminate any possibility of being caught unprepared by any material future risk or challenge.

It is helpful to summarize the results of our *Strategic Future Anticipation* activities in graphic form to facilitate the discussion and monitoring of relevant future scenarios (see chart 23). The user can employ different colors to plot different scenarios in this matrix (green dots for scenarios for which we are prepared, yellow dots for scenarios for which we are still preparing, and red dots for scenarios for which we are not yet prepared).

Chart 23: Strategic Risk-Opportunity Radar Screen

Please note that Strategic Future Anticipation is concerned only with future scenarios of strategic relevance either as a significant risk or an attractive opportunity. Diluting the concept with too many irrelevant scenarios is not helpful. In fact, doing so raises the risk of being distracted from severe risks and highly attractive opportunities. Less experienced clients often confuse frequency of risks with severity of risks. A frequent, but not severe, risk is nothing to worry about in the context of Strategic Future Anticipation. What we do worry about are the risks that occur infrequently, but have the ability to inflict existential damage (e.g., a severe financial crisis, job loss in a severe recession).

> **Caveat:** One should be aware that it may be difficult to decide whether a severe scenario is a risk or an opportunity. For example, for the well prepared, a major risk that weakens unprepared competitors becomes an attractive opportunity. Preparedness can turn severe risks into opportunities (in chart 23, these events move from left to right).

Unfortunately, even big corporations often fail to create or properly maintain such radar screens. They focus on one scenario (base case scenario) to which they devote their efforts, exposing them to many severe risks for which they lack even basic preparedness.

Strategic Future Anticipation, if conducted diligently, leads to the strategies required to raise preparedness to sufficient levels. Often, even simple actions lead to substantial improvement of overall preparedness.

For example, in 2012 many companies and individuals in the coastal areas of the northeastern United States failed to prepare for a major hurricane. This is astonishing, given the frequent warnings by experts.

In the aftermath of Hurricane Sandy, it was shocking to witness the low level of preparedness. Many people put themselves in danger by not having basic pre- and post-hurricane preparation in place, such as window protection, solar cell phone chargers, transistor radios, batteries, flashlights, and food and water supplies.

THE ULTIMATE GOAL: ACHIEVING TOTAL STRATEGIC PREPAREDNESS

When I talk to clients about *Total Strategic Preparedness*, they often claim to be sufficiently prepared. Even after suffering defeats and setbacks, clients refuse to admit to being unprepared. Such a defense mechanism is dangerous as it blocks learning from past mistakes and thus raises the chances for future unpreparedness and vulnerability.

For example, after the last financial crisis, many top executives of financial institutions claimed that the crisis was extremely unlikely and therefore unpredictable. Often, they called it a six-sigma event, a statistical term for extremely unlikely outcomes. The reality is different. The event was anything but unpredictable. There were a number of experts who warned of a crisis using credible fact-based analysis. There were some hedge fund managers and investors who prepared diligently for these circumstances that others claimed to be unpredictable. Applying critical thinking would have increased their preparedness to acceptable levels.

Unfortunately, finding excuses is too often the default mode of dealing with failures caused by negligent preparedness. We fail to use critical thinking to prepare for outcomes that deviate from our base case scenarios or our expectations; when disasters strike, we resort to finding excuses and blaming others for our own shortcomings.

In my experience working with top executives and investors internationally, I have witnessed great differences in the way winners and losers prepare for future volatility. Unfortunately, most people fail to understand and to value good preparedness.

To illustrate the difference between good and poor preparedness, I encourage clients to do the following exercise:

Quick exercise on understanding good preparedness: The *60-100-85 percent tool* for better preparedness and more success

Step 1: Assess your past preparedness for a failed project

Pick a past failure or unsuccessful outcome, such as an unsuccessful pitch for new business with an important client, a missed promotion, or any failed project.

Step 2: Define the case of perfect (100 %) preparedness

Use diligent critical thinking to dissect what went wrong. More specifically, create a list of all activities required to reach a state of perfect preparedness (100 %) for the past failure. In other words, imagine what would have constituted perfect preparedness in a perfect world.

To make the exercise more powerful, imagine that failure would have drastic consequences (e.g., job loss). This dramatization is often needed to break through the mindset of average preparedness and to open up to more radical ideas of what is needed for perfect preparedness.

> **Step 3: Assess your actual preparedness**
>
> Compare the activities required for perfect preparedness with your actual level of preparedness preceding your failure. Most often, the actual level of preparedness reached 60 % at best. In other words, you could have done much better.
>
> **Step 4: Going forward, strive for 85 % preparedness**
>
> Now focus on a current project or challenge. List all activities needed for perfect preparedness and compare the list to your traditional way of preparing for a project or challenge (the 60 % case). Make a decision to leave the 60 % world and target at least a level of 85 % preparedness (i.e. aim at surpassing the middle point between traditional and perfect preparedness).[26]

After conducting this exercise (i.e., after understanding the gap between their actual and perfect preparedness), participants often realize that most often it is their lack of preparedness that is responsible for their suboptimal outcomes or failures in life. It is common that participants rate their own past preparedness at levels of 60 % or lower. Please note that the goal is not to have perfect preparedness all the time. Such ambitious goals are not realistic. The advice I give clients in workshops and presentations is that, if you manage to raise your preparedness from 60% to 85 % (i.e. slightly more than the midpoint between traditional and perfect preparedness), you will see a significant increase in overall success.

To ensure that our preparedness strategies are at the required standard, we should test them against the following criteria:

1. **Effectivity**: Our preparedness strategies must effectively address possible challenges presented by a wide variety of different developments and scenarios.
2. **Efficiency**: The costs of implementing these preparedness strategies must be reasonable compared to the magnitude and severity of threats or opportunities.

3. **Completeness**: Preparedness strategies must provide comprehensive protection against disruptions, risks, and the unexpected.
4. **Timing**: Preparedness strategies should be in place ahead of time.

When we critically review our current preparedness against these requirements, we may detect serious shortcomings. The concept of *Total Strategic Preparedness* offers a structured and coordinated approach to perfect preparedness.

Total Strategic Preparedness rests on three requirements, the three pillars of *Total Strategic Preparedness* (see chart 24). The first pillar is defensive, requiring early identification and mitigation of risk scenarios. The second pillar is proactive, seeking to leverage our defensive preparedness and knowledge into decisive strategic advantages vis-à-vis competitors. The final pillar is offensive and seeks to create disruptions and surprises for which our competitors are unprepared. In other words, we become the disruptor in an unprepared market place or environment.

Each pillar may lead to significantly better outcomes. However, the best results will be achieved by excelling in all three pillars simultaneously.

Chart 24: The three pillars of Total Strategic Preparedness

| Defensive Pillar: Anticipate major risks | Proactive Pillar: Exploit own preparedness | Disruptive Pillar: Become a disruptor |

The first pillar is the most important as it seeks to immunize us against risks for which we are not prepared. This is traditional risk management. Past successes are meaningless if we get hit by a severe risk event that was not on our risk radar screen. It takes just one single risk event to turn a long lasting success story into a spectacular failure.

For example, many investors accumulated great wealth by aggressively investing in U.S. residential real estate or related securities between 1996 and 2005. Many suffered extremely painful losses when they failed to prepare for falling home prices. For many, the losses of this one single risk event wiped out all previous gains.

Similarly, smartphone maker Blackberry lost its industry leadership when caught unprepared by Apple's market entry in 2007. It took one competitor with one innovative product to end a great success story. The functionality of Apple's new iPhone caught Blackberry and many other manufacturers by surprise and led to significant losses of market share and revenues.

Ensuring defensive preparedness is extremely important. Defensive preparedness starts with using critical thinking to create a complete spectrum of possible outcomes and developments and an analysis of their impact on the present. The focus is on the "what could go wrong" scenarios.

Rather than trying to predict the exact course of the future and focusing on one scenario, defensive preparedness uses critical thinking to identify the spectrum of all relevant scenarios, assesses their impact, and devises preparedness strategies. This is completely different from most companies' and individuals' approaches to risks and opportunity management.

Developing the spectrum of potential scenarios must be as complete as possible, using brainstorming sessions, expert interviews, targeted workshops with external support (e.g., experts, experienced moderators), case studies, and targeted study of research. It is extremely important to include the expertise of people who do not share our views. Chances are high that people who disagree with us will help us to achieve completeness when constructing our risk radar screen.

Defensive preparedness should never be taken for granted. It needs to be reviewed and stress tested by continuous use of critical thinking tools and concepts.

After securing our defensive preparedness, we move to the second pillar of the *Total Strategic Preparedness* framework: proactive preparedness. The goal is to leverage our defensive preparedness and intelligence to devise proactive strategies that provide a competitive edge or the potential for substantial value creation.

A good example of proactive preparedness can be found in Michael Lewis' *The Big Short*. Lewis describes a group of fund managers who in the early 2000s detected a severe threat to the financial system. These investors ensured they would not suffer significant losses if such a crisis occurred (defensive preparedness). They did not stop at defensive preparedness. They created investment strategies that would provide opportunities if the crisis did occur. The combination of defensive and proactive preparedness worked extremely well and generated substantial profits for the group of investors portrayed in Lewis' book. They turned risks into attractive opportunities.

Another example of combining defensive and proactive preparedness is investor Warren Buffett. For more than fifty years, Buffett has been extremely successful in implementing the first two pillars of *Total Strategic Preparedness*. His superb preparedness for the many disruptions in the economy and financial markets made him one of the wealthiest individuals in the world. Despite the enormous volatility and disruption in the economy and financial markets, Buffett managed not only to protect himself (defensive preparedness), but also to turn many of the most severe risk events into moneymaking opportunities (proactive preparedness).

His performance during the U.S. inflation crisis of the 1970s is legendary and a great example of successful preparedness in a highly volatile and disruptive environment where many companies and investors suffered tremendous losses.

Case Study: Warren Buffett, a master of *Preparedness*

An excellent example of the power of preparedness is Warren Buffett, one of the most successful investors and businessmen in modern history. Financial crises and severe disruptions played a significant role in his success story. In fact, without financial crises, Buffett's performance would have been much less impressive.

Buffett made many (if not most) of his successful deals during times of severe financial and economic disruptions. He was better prepared than others to deal with the disruptions and the enormous risks that occurred during times of financial stress. Buffett managed to use the insights on which his defensive preparedness (i.e., protection against risks) was built to develop proactive investment strategies that profited from others' unpreparedness. This included stock investments, acquisitions, emergency bailouts, and financing of companies less prepared for the crisis.

One of the most impressive examples is Buffett's handling of the 1970s inflation crisis in the U.S. Even highly acclaimed economists were caught by surprise by a new phenomenon, stagflation (i.e., low economic growth coupled with high inflation). During this period, businesses were disrupted by two major inflation shocks and two severe recessions. Interest rates were moving wildly, reaching the twenty percent level at one point. The first inflation shock (1973-74) led to a fifty percent stock market correction.

The inflation period from 1973 to 1982 was one of the most severe crises in modern U.S. history. The performance of the S&P 500 was, adjusted for inflation, negative. Buffett's Berkshire Hathaway company, however, excelled during this dramatic period and achieved a phenomenal return of more than eight hundred percent for its investors.[27] This success was not accidental. An essay written by Buffett in 1976 on the economics of inflation clearly demonstrates his superb understanding of business economics during times of high inflation. Buffett was prepared for high inflation, when others were not. [28]

> What is particularly impressive about Buffett is that he managed to fulfill the requirements of *Total Strategic Preparedness* throughout a long career. This is remarkable as most success stories in modern business seem rather limited and do not last over multiple decades.

The last pillar of *Total Strategic Preparedness* requires us to move from a reactive mode (reacting to outside shocks and challenges) to an active one (creating disruptions). Disruptive preparedness is one of the most challenging strategies of the *Total Strategic Preparedness* framework. Those who pursue this strategy disrupt their industries and environments and create adverse surprises for others. They change the rules of the game and leverage their own preparedness for the new status quo.

Apple Computers is a good example of implementing the strategy of disruptive preparedness. The company is one of few that fulfills the requirements of all three pillars of *Total Strategic Preparedness*. Not surprisingly, Apple Computers is one of the most profitable and highly valued companies.

Let us discuss the Apple case study in more detail.[29] Apple is prepared to deal with disruptions and risks in the technology sector, fulfilling all requirements of defensive preparedness, pillar one.[30] Apple has used its defensive preparedness to launch successful proactive strategies such as "stealing" market share from competitors unprepared for the volatile technology environment (proactive preparedness, pillar two).

However, Apple is best known as a dangerous disruptor of the market of consumer electronics. The introduction of the iPod, the iPad, and the iPhone were best practice examples of successfully disrupting an industry and being best prepared for the consequences (disruptive preparedness, pillar three).

Developing strategies for disruptive preparedness is a demanding business activity. While it is easy to create disruptions (e.g., starting a dysfunctional price war), it is challenging to ensure that these disruptions are beneficial to the disruptor in the short <u>and</u> long term. Disruptors may profit from first-order consequences, but not from second- and third-order consequences for which they were not adequately prepared. A disruption may backfire. In world history, many countries that started "surprise wars" (disruptors) saw their strategies backfire terribly when the attacked countries developed new strategies or built powerful alliances. Equally, companies starting disruptive price wars or attacking foreign competitors' home markets may find themselves in trouble if they failed to be prepared fully for the long-term consequences of their disruptive strategies.[31]

Therefore, disruption without long-term defensive preparedness is not a viable strategy; it is excessively risky. Diligent critical thinking is required to achieve adequate levels of preparedness.

Online retailer Amazon is another good example of excelling at all three pillars of Total Strategic Preparedness. Amazon is a successful and experienced disruptor. Amazon was able to pursue disruptive strategies because of its impressive level of defensive preparedness. No competitor has yet replicated Amazon's success or weakened its competitive position.

Total Strategic Preparedness can be implemented in different ways. Warren Buffett is an example of focusing almost exclusively on pillar one (defensive preparedness) and pillar two (proactive preparedness) strategies. Technology companies such as Apple and Amazon exemplify the generation of competitive advantage by pursuing pillar three strategies (disruptive preparedness), while securing past and current success with superb defensive preparedness. There are many strategic interpretations of *Total Strategic Preparedness*. However, there is one mandatory requirement: Defensive *Preparedness* is never negotiable. It is a must if you want long-term success.

FIVE REQUIREMENTS FOR TOTAL STRATEGIC PREPAREDNESS

Total Strategic Preparedness is a highly desirable state that few individuals, teams, and organizations achieve. However, preparedness is not a hot topic in business. It is rarely discussed in management text books nor seen on board meeting agendas.

This is surprising, given its huge potential for value creation and long-term success. Therefore, raising one's preparedness should be the starting point for any strategic initiative seeking higher levels of success.

There are at least five key principles for achieving *Total Strategic Preparedness* (see chart 25).

Chart 25: Five principles required for *Total Strategic Preparedness*

FIVE PRINCIPLES FOR *TOTAL STRATEGIC PREPAREDNESS*
1. The need to worry
2. Strive for comprehensive preparedness. Remember: a single instance of unpreparedness can wipe out past successes.
3. Do not try to time the arrival of a major risk event or disruption; instead, prepare for it ASAP. (Do not procrastinate!)
4. Invert your view of risks and opportunities. View risks as opportunities and opportunities as risks.
5. Understand the direct link of critical thinking, preparedness, and long-term success and act accordingly.

First Principle: The need to worry

Critical thinking requires constant constructive worry about future challenges and our preparedness. It is not only acceptable to worry; it is highly desirable to do so. Do not get distracted by the army of positive thinkers and their battle cry, "Don't worry. Be happy." Successful people do worry. They know that worrying is an effective stress test of their own preparedness for future challenges, risks, and disruptions. Constructive worrying will help you find your own vulnerabilities; confidence and exuberance will not.

Unfortunately, the world does not operate like this; most people do exactly the opposite. With strong belief in positive thinking, they assume that everything will turn out fine. Worry is seen as either a weakness or an unwanted psychological trait. However, keep in mind that positive thinking is nothing more than a dangerously biased view of reality, resulting in an unjustified comfortable state of mind, unprepared for adverse future developments. In the short term, this may lead to a state of "happy unsuccessfulness"; in the long term, happiness may turn into frustration and disappointments.

Therefore, positive thinking is not only incompatible with critical thinking, but also with the goal of preparedness.

Admittedly, not all worry is constructive. Too often worries turn into depression or paralysis. Constructive worrying seeks to improve our situation by engaging in targeted proactive action. It aims at eliminating or reducing adverse surprises. It is a character trait of highly successful individuals (see below) but uncommon among average and poor performers.

The need to worry – a business anecdote

A few years ago, one of the most successful investors in the world was interviewed on Bloomberg television. The reporter pointed out that stock prices were up, interest rates were down, economic growth rebounding, and credit easy to obtain. He then asked the investor, "Given all these positive developments, is there anything you worry about in the current world?" The investor looked puzzled and I recollect him saying something like: "Young man, I worry all the time. I never stop worrying. That is why I am so successful."

Second Principle: Strive for comprehensive preparedness. Remember: a single instance of unpreparedness can wipe out past successes

Preparedness is a tricky concept. One moment of unpreparedness can turn a long-term success story into a monumental failure. A successful business can be wiped out by a single risk event. An investor can lose all his wealth if a scenario occurs for which he is unprepared. A highly rated soccer team can lose an important match if surprised by an opponent's innovative strategy.

Preparedness requires obsession with completeness. Even a ninety-five percent preparedness score can leave us dangerously exposed to severe risks. When we deal with severe, existential risks, this is not acceptable. For example, upgrading all windows of a Florida home to hurricane protection standards is not enough if the front door is not equally secure. A single vulnerability during a hurricane can destroy your house. Preparedness for severe risks requires completeness.

Therefore, it is mandatory to constantly stress test one's preparedness for severe, existential risks. Invite others to challenge your level of preparedness. Invite the best critical thinkers you know to find gaps in your preparedness strategy.

This is particularly important during times of well-being and overconfidence. Preparedness typically is most needed when dismissed as irrelevant and a waste of time. Therefore, when times are calm and peaceful for an extended period, it is mandatory to raise your level of preparedness.

Third Principle: Do not try to time the arrival of a major risk event or disruption; prepare for it ASAP (Do not procrastinate!)

Do not postpone activities that raise your level of preparedness. The attitude "I will start my preparation closer to the arrival of a risk event" is a sure path to disaster. You can anticipate major risk events, but you cannot precisely time them. You may get away with this for a short time (i.e., be lucky), but in the long-term this is a dangerous path to follow.

Accurately predicting severe risk events is close to impossible. Most risk events have a human component. Typically, they are the result of a critical mass of people moving from irrational to rational thinking. For example, the financial crisis of 2007 was caused by people believing that U.S. home prices could only rise in the foreseeable future (irrational thinking) changing their minds to believe that a reversal of home prices was imminent (rational thinking). The exact timing for such a thought reversal is impossible to predict accurately.

Consequently, we should not waste resources predicting the exact timing of risk events, but focus on preparing for them ASAP. We may prepare for risk events that never materialize, but this is part of a good preparedness strategy. It is a powerful insurance policy needed before a risk event takes place. Preparing for a risk event that does not occur is not a waste of resources. It is sophisticated risk management.

Fourth Principle: Invert your view of risks and opportunities. View risks as opportunities and opportunities as risks.

Many people view risks and opportunities as two different and unrelated events that require different preparedness strategies. Such a view is misleading because our level of preparedness often determines whether an event turns out to be a risk or an opportunity.

In competitive situations, we gain an advantage (opportunity) if we are better prepared for a risk event than our competitors (unless the risk event is so great as to wipe out both the prepared and unprepared). Therefore, risks are often camouflaged opportunities to gain a significant competitive advantage or to make a fortune by being better prepared than others. Risks are particularly attractive in situations of widespread collective unpreparedness. In those circumstances, risks can become exceptional opportunities for the prepared.

Opportunities, on the other hand, are often camouflaged risks. This can occur in at least two different circumstances. First, we miss an emerging opportunity that disrupts our marketplace and rewards our competitors who are prepared. Second, opportunities pursued by many often turn into a misperception of reality. When too many chase a single opportunity, it may disappear, leaving significant risk (see chart 26). Therefore, opportunities pursued by many should trigger our risk management defense systems.

Chart 26: Opportunities that turned out to be camouflaged risks (examples)

OPPORTUNITIES THAT TURNED OUT TO BE CAMOUFLAGED RISKS
• Internet stock boom before the peak of 2002 • U.S. housing market before the peak of 2006-2007 • Boom of credit derivatives prior to 2007 • Asbestos use as fire retardant during the 1970s • Foreign currency mortgages/loans before reversal of foreign exchange rates • Most large acquisitions in the business world, particularly at the end of an economic boom period

Fifth Principle: Understand the direct link of critical thinking, preparedness, and long-term success and act accordingly.

As long as we remember the connection between critical thinking, better preparedness, and more successful outcomes, we are well prepared to deal with future risks, disruptions, and emerging opportunities.

The level of preparedness is often the key difference between long-term high and low performers. This is true in all situations. We must ensure sufficient levels of preparedness compatible with our ambitions. Therefore, pursuing higher risk strategies requires higher levels of preparedness. The *Total Strategic Preparedness* concept systematically stress tests our level of preparedness and strategies for improvement. The concept can be used in both professional and personal life and is one of the easiest success enablers available, particularly when we are experienced in using it.

Keep in mind: adverse surprises in our lives are signs for preparedness deficits. If you strive for higher levels of success, you must work on these deficits. Otherwise, you may end up as one of the countless boom-bust examples.

Summary:

In this chapter, the following tools, frameworks, and concepts are discussed:

- Preparedness
- *Total Strategic Preparedness* including
    - *defensive preparedness*
    - *proactive preparedness*
    - *disruptive preparedness*
- Five principles for achieving *Total Strategic Preparedness*
- *Strategic Future Anticipation*
- *Crisis of unpreparedness*
- *Risk-opportunity radar screen*
- The *60-100-85 percent preparedness tool*

Exercises:

Exercise 1: Review past successes and failures

Select three situations in which you were successful and three situations in which you suffered a major setback. Using the concepts discussed in this chapter, analyze the quality of your preparedness for each situation. What are the lessons learned for the future?

Exercise 2: Look for positive and negative examples

Pick three examples of successful organizations, teams, groups, or individuals. Analyze their preparedness using the concepts presented here. Repeat the exercise focusing on three examples of organizations, teams, groups, or individuals that suffered major setbacks. Do the levels of preparedness explain the outcomes?

Exercise 3: Improve your level of preparedness going forward

Apply the concept of *Total Strategic Preparedness* to your own life. For each type of preparedness (i.e., defensive, proactive, and disruptive), list five or more activities that will improve your preparedness for risks, disruptions, and opportunities.

CHAPTER 5 - THE BLUE BELT: DIFFERENT PROBLEMS REQUIRE DIFFERENT APPROACHES TO THINKING

When we consider thinking in general, and critical thinking in particular, we are often vague about what we mean by thinking and how we go about it. There are many different approaches to thinking. Just as we need a specific screwdriver depending on the size and type of a screw, we need a different approach to thinking depending on the type of the problem or situation we are facing. Selecting the right approach can dramatically improve the success of our critical thinking activities.

Many companies and individuals fail at this. They believe that one screwdriver is all they need, leading to inefficiency, ineffectiveness, frustration, and, eventually, failure.

The solution is simple. We should know what we want to accomplish and then choose the most appropriate approach. This chapter introduces eight approaches for directing and organizing thinking activities (see chart 27). There are many more approaches available, but these are a good start.

Chart 27: Different Approaches to Thinking[32]

Perspective-Based Thinking	Consequential Thinking
• Encourages us to look at a problem or situation from different perspectives to generate new insights	• Asks us to consider in great detail the short- and long-term consequences of a decision or action
Situational Thinking	**Strategic Thinking**
• Seeks to gain a detailed understanding of the situational context before making important decisions. Recognizes that unique situations require tailor-made solutions	• Develops a plan of well-coordinated actions and decisions to gain a competitive advantage
Anticipatory Thinking	**Innovative Thinking**
• Seeks to anticipate future risks and opportunities to improve preparedness and avoid adverse surprises	• Develops new solutions to improve current situations or solve significant problems and challenges
Systemic Thinking	**Stress Testing**
• Uses a macroscopic view to map connectivity, interdependency, and interfaces of complex systems before making important decisions	• Reviews existing solutions, processes, and practices to test their resilience to major stress events

PERSPECTIVE-BASED THINKING

In the movie "Dead Poets Society," an unconventional teacher encourages his students at a 1950s boarding school to step on top of their classroom desks to gain a different perspective of the world. It is a lesson in the importance of changing perspectives when judging the world around us.

Adopting appropriate perspectives is a prerequisite to successful critical thinking. Before we draw a conclusion, we need to look at the situation from all relevant views. Changing perspectives almost always leads to new insights, enabling us to make better decisions. The following example underlines the importance of perspective in critical thinking.

The importance of perspective (case example)
A management consultant is invited to an off-site strategy session of an investment bank. He arrives early and listens to the strategic discussions of the bankers. What he hears shocks him. The bankers talk for two hours about strategy without using the word "client," or important topics such as clients' needs and preferences. Instead, their discussions focus on incentive systems and how their bonuses should be calculated. When it was the management consultant's turn to speak about industry trends, he shared his observation with the audience. The bankers were both surprised and embarrassed. They failed to consider the most important perspective when crafting their future strategy, that of the client.

Adopting a single or inappropriate perspective is a sure way to sabotage critical thinking. Decisions derived from such a poor foundation are likely to result in suboptimal outcomes.

The investment bankers in the above example failed to understand that adopting the perspective of their clients should have been the starting point and main focus of their strategic discussions. Instead, they jumped to the issue that was most important to them: the calculation and size of the bonus pool and their compensation. Focusing on clients leads to better product and service offerings, which would have meant more revenues and higher bonuses in the long term.

It is important to adopt several different perspectives when assessing a challenging situation or problem. For example, Central Banks should adopt multiple perspectives before making any policy decisions (e.g., raising or lowering interest rates). They must look at the world from the perspectives of consumers, debtors, creditors, companies, and investors. Similarly, business managers need to adopt the perspectives of customers, employees, competitors, investors, and regulators. Decisions improve exponentially with the number of adopted perspectives.

Changing perspective is also an important tool in solving social conflicts. Forcing the parties to consider each other's perspective may lead to conflict resolution. This is true on a macrolevel (conflicts between countries) and on a microlevel (conflicts between individuals).

CONSEQUENTIAL THINKING

One of the biggest challenges of successful critical thinking is to anticipate correctly short- and long-term consequences of a decision or action. Consequential thinking forces us to address this issue.

In a previous chapter, *The Law of the 4.5th Consequence* was introduced to provide a structure for consequential thinking. This tool forces us to anticipate the chain of consequences that result from our decisions and actions. Refer to chapter three for more information on this topic.

Consequential thinking is important when we operate in complex, intertwined systems found in politics, economics, business, and society. The number and relevance of complex systems has increased dramatically over the past decades. Therefore, consequential thinking will improve the quality of our decisions.

SITUATIONAL THINKING

Politicians and celebrities often wear custom-made clothes tailored to adjust to body characteristics. While expensive due to the manual labor required, the results are often impressive.

The same principle is true for our thinking. Every situation is as unique as our bodies. A person borrowing a tailor-made suit does not look as good wearing it as the original owner. Similarly, we cannot copy strategies or solutions developed for other situations and presume to have the same success. Situational contexts are rarely the same; we must adjust our thinking to the uniqueness of a situation or problem. The copy paste strategy does not work in the real world. Therefore, critical thinking activities must pay attention to the situational context.

Many less successful companies do not understand this important lesson. They hire expensive consultants who present strategies of an industry leader, hoping that copying a leader's strategy will make their clients as successful. This widespread practice is referred to as competitive benchmarking.

People who follow this approach fail to understand that there are great differences among companies, including culture, skill, people, experience, risk appetite, attitude, and process. Even if a company succeeded in copying an industry leader, by the time it has, it is too late. A new situational context has emerged and the industry leader will have adopted a new strategy addressing the demands of a new reality. The copier will be left with an outdated strategy.

> **Personal Example**
>
> In more than twenty years of consulting and advisory work, I have never witnessed an industry leader hiring a consultant for competitive benchmarking. This is not of concern to industry leaders. That is why they are industry leaders. Their work is related to anticipating future risks and opportunities. They are not interested in copying others.
>
> I have had the opportunity to spend many years with a company that is recognized as a leader in its field. This company did not study its competitors. It strived to understand and serve its clients, not copy its competitors. The same is true of one of the most successful companies in the world, Apple Computers. Since the return of co-founder Steve Jobs, the company has concentrated on developing the best and most innovative products. I doubt that Jobs spent any time copying others.

Our thinking produces the best results when we focus on the situational context in which we are operating. We can learn much from the past, but if we do not consider situational contexts, we are likely to fail.

Understanding the situational context in which we operate can be achieved by studying and mapping the most relevant parameters and factors. Chart 28 describes a set of parameters that must be analyzed and considered for a complete understanding of the situational context.

Chart 28: Parameters of the situational context of a business decision – simplified case example

Analyzing the situational context: Relevant parameters for an investment decision	
<ul><li>Interest rates (outlook)</li><li>Tax situation</li><li>Strategic priorities</li><li>Risk appetite</li><li>Investors' preferences</li><li>Competitors' strategies</li><li>Projected market growth</li><li>Future risks/disruptions</li><li>Own skill/experience portfolio</li></ul>	<ul><li>Central bank policies (now, future)</li><li>Credit rating and financing costs</li><li>Legal framework (present/future)</li><li>Regulatory framework</li><li>Political situation</li><li>Foreign exchange rates</li></ul>

Making decisions without understanding the situational context in which we operate puts us at great risk and is not compatible with critical thinking.

STRATEGIC THINKING

It is difficult to achieve long-term success without strategic thinking. Well thought out strategies aimed at a decisive competitive advantage or material value generation are the foundation of all success.

There are inflated and often incorrect uses of the terms strategy and strategic. Not every plan is a strategy. Strategy refers to a well-coordinated set of activities and decisions derived from rigorous analyses that strive to secure a decisive competitive advantage or achieve a meaningful goal.

Strategy is a military term that comes from the Greek word "strategos," referring to a military leader charged with planning and conducting military activities.[33]

Strategic thinking can be used in both competitive and noncompetitive situations. In the former, we are mainly concerned with winning and moving ahead of competitors. A soccer coach will craft a strategy for his team to win the World Cup. The strategy uses given resources in a specific situational context in the most efficient and effective way to secure a favorable outcome (i.e., winning the tournament).

In noncompetitive situations, strategic thinking is used to achieve a meaningful goal or to generate material value. A mountain climber uses strategic thinking to ascend safely and efficiently to the top of a mountain. His strategy is a coordinated set of decisions covering topics such as timing, team composition, route, equipment, and risk management.

There is substantial difference between strategic thinking in competitive and in noncompetitive situations. In the former, there are at least four requirements:

1. Our strategies must be kept secret from our competitors.
2. We must develop strategic surprises that catch our competitors unprepared.
3. We must be prepared to deal with our competitors' strategic surprises.
4. Our strategies must change over time to prevent our competitors from anticipating our moves.

In addition, there are some general requirements for strategies and strategic thinking that apply to noncompetitive situations:

- Our strategies must perform well over the short- and long-term.
- Our strategies should not expose us to risks outside of our risk tolerance or risk appetite spectrum.

- Our strategies must be capable of implementation given the available resources.
- Strategies must not be weakened by groupthink, political consensus, or other activities that place social cohesiveness and feel-good factors ahead of the best possible decisions.
- Our strategies must use our resources efficiently and effectively.

The outcome of strategic thinking sessions is improved significantly by including experienced and skilled consultants. For example, when formulating the strategy for the difficult ascent of a mountain, it is helpful to seek the advice of mountaineers who have climbed this mountain and are familiar with the geography. Good strategies are based on the input of many experts. However, in most cases, the final strategic decisions are made by a single person or a small group.

Strategic thinking requires rigorous and dedicated analyses to reach meaningful conclusions. A strategy that lacks a sufficient analytical foundation is likely to do more harm than good.

ANTICIPATORY THINKING

Anticipatory thinking is employed when making decisions for an uncertain future. There are two main goals that can be accomplished by using anticipatory thinking. First, this type of thinking can help reduce adverse surprises. Adverse surprises are always a sign of unpreparedness and a lack of critical thinking (i.e., anticipatory thinking). Negative surprises lead to setbacks, losses, and other bad outcomes. Second, anticipatory thinking can be used to gain competitive advantage by being better prepared to deal with future disruptions, risks, or newly emerging opportunities than our competitors.

Anticipatory thinking can be used in almost all situations that deal with an uncertain future, including:

- A company preparing a five-year strategic plan
- A family planning finances and life cycle events (financing children's college tuition, retirement)
- A student planning a professional career

Anticipatory thinking involves preparing for future events. The previous chapter discusses the concept of preparedness, important to anticipatory thinking. Refer to that discussion for more detailed information.

Future uncertainty can be substantially reduced by anticipatory thinking (see chart 29) for two reasons. First, future outcomes are often a consequence of present actions and trends. Understanding our current situations in great detail is an enormous help to anticipate potential future outcomes.

For example, rising indebtedness leads to specific future challenges (e.g., risk exposure to rising interest rates, spending limits due to interest rate and principal payments). A highly indebted society is likely to experience future problems. These problems can be anticipated.

Second, rigorous anticipatory thinking can identify future disruptions, risks, and opportunities. Identifying such scenarios helps in devising proactive strategies to improve preparedness, and avoiding painful or costly setbacks and losses. Preparedness helps us deal with an uncertain future, reducing negative surprises (see chart 29).

Chart 29: *Anticipatory Thinking* makes life more predictable (illustrative example)

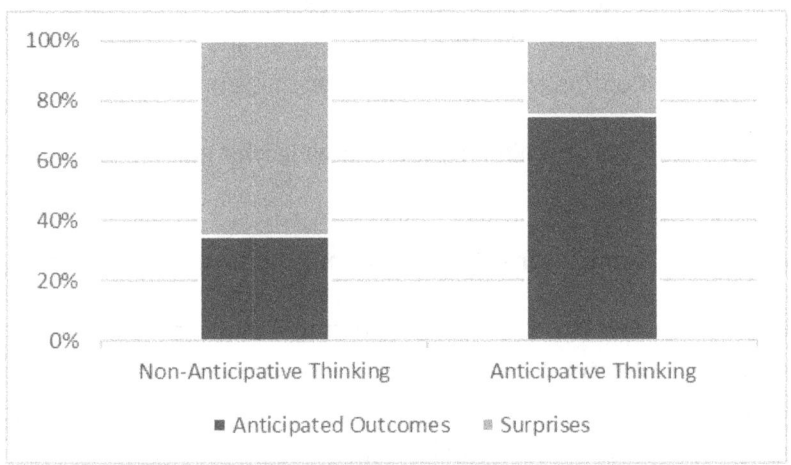

The key to successful anticipatory thinking is to focus on possible future scenarios (what **could** be) and not on predictions of the future (what **will** be). While we can answer the question "What could be?" by anticipatory thinking and coming up with a range of possible scenarios, we typically fail to predict the exact future course of events.

Anticipatory thinking encourages us to consider the spectrum of risks and opportunities (what **could** be). It discourages us from attempting to predict the future (what **will** be), a dramatic difference. Here is an example.

Those living in Florida need to worry about hurricanes. Using anticipatory thinking, we create a list of preparations to minimize the damages and losses from a direct hit. These measures include protecting our house (e.g., install impact windows or shutters, fix loose roof tiles, cut down trees), stockpiling food, water, batteries, flashlights, transistor radio, medications, and other items. Diligent anticipatory thinking can put us in the best possible state of preparedness for such a risk scenario. However, it would not help predict the exact day and time of a future hurricane, its route, or strength. It is useless to attempt such predictions.

Anticipatory thinking is easier today than in the past. The availability of data has improved exponentially with modern technologies such as the internet. However, the mass of available data may distract us from conducting the correct analyses. We must focus on data and information that is relevant to our situation to increase our level of preparedness.

To implement anticipatory thinking, the following four guiding principles are useful:

Guiding Principle Number One: Recognize that the future is not linear

Assuming that future outcomes are linear extrapolations of recent trends is a sure path to disaster. Trends stop, reverse, are disrupted, and are replaced by new ones. What is important is to anticipate what deviations from recent trends could occur and how they could impact us.

Equally important is to understand that the future is not always better than the past. Times may be worse for an extended period. For example, people in Germany in 1913 may have thought of the future as bright and prosperous. Few would have correctly anticipated that the country would endure two major world wars, hyperinflation, collapsing currency, hunger, and a barbaric dictatorship. Optimism bias tends to prevent people from anticipating negative future scenarios, even when warnings signs are clearly visible.

Excluding negative scenarios or assessing them as extremely unlikely is a sure way to be caught unprepared when a risk event happens. We must resist the temptation of positive thinking and linear trend extrapolation when preparing for the future.

Guiding Principle Number Two: Understand anticipatory thinking and the differences between macroenvironment and microenvironment

We employ anticipatory thinking to learn more about the future environment and those differences between our macroenvironment (country, state) and our microenvironment (job, house).

Obviously, both environments are of crucial importance. We cannot influence our macroenvironment. Whether a country's economy grows or slides into recession, we cannot affect. We can, however, greatly influence, shape, and change our microenvironment. For example, our professional career is greatly dependent on securing relevant and marketable skills. Anticipatory thinking can identify the skills likely to be in demand going forward.

Most people are unaware of their micro future's dependence on their own actions and decisions. They fail to use anticipatory thinking to identify the actions needed to achieve better outcomes. In other words, we greatly shape our microenvironment either through active decision making or through our own passivity. Our macroenvironment, however, is outside of our influence zone. All we can do is to leave an unattractive macroenvironment by relocating to a different state or country. In fact, doing so was often a great strategy in world history.

Guiding Principle Number Three: Allocate sufficient quality time to anticipatory thinking

Most people and organizations spend too little time on anticipatory thinking, missing the chance to secure a better future. When we track the time individuals think about the past, the present, and the future, we are likely to arrive at the results shown in chart 30. Most of our thinking is allocated to the present and the past. Only a fraction of our time is devoted to anticipatory thinking.

Chart 30: Allocation of thinking time for average or less successful people (estimates based on actual observations)

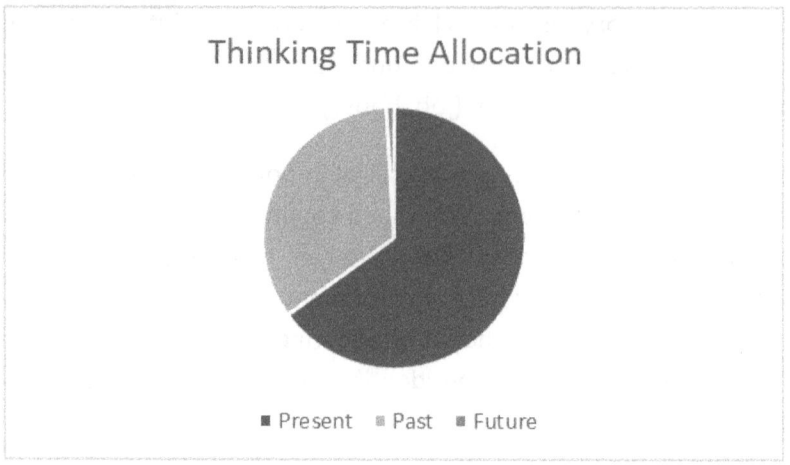

When I present this chart, most people protest and claim it does not reflect them. Admittedly, it is a subjective estimate based on a small sample.[34] However, a one percent allocation to anticipatory thinking (i.e., quality reflection on risks and opportunities that could occur in five or more years) translates into roughly three and a half days of thinking exclusively about the future. I doubt that many people reserve three and a half days per year exclusively to reflect about the future.

Thinking about the past and the present is not necessarily a bad thing. If we reflect on the past with the intention of identifying specific lessons learned or life principles, this time is well spent. However, our thinking about the past is often spent reminiscing about good times or lamenting bad times. When those who are fifty year of age or older are asked whether anticipatory thinking could have prevented some of their bad outcomes, they readily agree. Many recite long lists of bad outcomes (career, family, and financial issues) that easily could have been prevented by anticipatory thinking.

Therefore, it is important to devote sufficient time to anticipatory thinking, perhaps dedicating time in your calendar.

Guiding Principle Number Four: The importance of asking questions

Many clients have asked me for specific outlines on how to conduct anticipatory thinking sessions. Obviously, companies do not want their anticipatory sessions to degrade into science fiction fantasies or unguided and wild brainstorming.

The best starting point is to use questions to challenge your current conduct and thinking critically. Chart 31 shows a selection of questions to start a personal anticipatory thinking session. Similarly, a list of starter questions can be compiled for companies. Most management consultancies use questions when working with clients on topics related to the future. They do not know the answers to these questions. They use them to start the process to get to the right answers.

Chart 31: Starter questions for *Anticipatory Thinking*: personal planning example

USING ANTICIPATORY THINKING FOR PERSONAL PLANNING: SAMPLE STARTER QUESTIONS
<ul><li>What is my current skill portfolio and how relevant will my skills be in the future (in five, ten years)?</li><li>Which skills will be in demand? Do I have these skills?</li><li>How secure is my job, position, company? Where would I work if I lost my job today, next month, or next year?</li><li>Am I easily replaceable at my current job? If yes, how can I change this?</li><li>What financial resources are needed over the next five to twenty years to maintain my current standard of living given education and health care costs, retirement? Will I have the required financial resources?</li><li>How will my current lifestyle choices such as nutrition and exercise impact my health in five, ten, and twenty years?</li><li>How safe and prosperous will my city, state, and country be in five, ten, and twenty years? Should I consider relocation?</li><li>What adverse scenarios could seriously impact my personal stability, financial situation, and professional career? What preparatory actions should I perform to mitigate these risks?</li></ul>

The key to successful anticipatory thinking is to question everything: beliefs, assumptions about life and the future, recent trends, and current strengths and weaknesses. The more radical the questions, the better the insights leading to wise decisions and successful outcomes.

INNOVATIVE THINKING

Innovative thinking is required when we are looking for new solutions and approaches to current or future problems, processes, and situations. Innovations disrupt the status quo and can be powerful vehicles for becoming more successful.

Countless books have been written on how countries, organizations, teams, and individuals can be more innovative. However, there is no simple recipe.

During my career as a management consultant and investment banker, I have worked closely with many innovative people. Based on my observations and experiences, I have developed the following set of factors that might help to practice innovative thinking.

Factor 1: The importance of critical observation

The belief that innovations are created by a single intuition or a flash of genius is often wrong. Innovations are often the result of intense critical observation. Critical observation is an important topic that will be discussed in more detail in chapter 8. Critical observation refers to a dedicated and intense observation and monitoring of the world. This includes the observation and the study of rules, patterns, anomalies, correlations, interdependencies, trends, and many other relevant items.

The American inventor Charles Kettering is said to have claimed, "A problem thoroughly understood is always fairly simple."[35] Critical observation contributes to the thorough understanding of a problem and can be considered an important launch pad for innovations.

Factor 2: Breaking free from limiting constraints

Innovators need to break free from constraints that limit their thinking and imagination. If we are stuck in the traditional world, we are unlikely to come up with new solutions. We should be ready to revise, question, and possibly suspend our current beliefs, assumptions, processes, perspectives, definitions, and structures.

Factor 3: The breadth and depth of our experience and knowledge

There are examples of innovations from people who were not experts in their fields. Based on my experience, these are exceptions. Successful innovators typically possess great expertise in their areas. Technology innovations are likely to be developed by those in this field, as medical breakthroughs are likely made by the medically trained.

There are two reasons why experts are more likely to come up with innovations. First, knowledge and expertise enable us to draw relevant analogies, which give important clues for innovative search. Second, extensive knowledge and experience foster the assessment of a new idea or hypothesis, avoiding time wasted.

Becoming an expert in a field does not necessarily require a university degree. Anyone can become an expert in any field through disciplined study.

Factor 4: The number of trials

Not every attempt to create an innovation is successful; many attempts fail, even for serial innovators. In a famous TED-x speech, cognitive psychologist Adam Grant points out that the greatest musical composers also produced the greatest number of musical pieces.[36] The more we try, the more likely it is that we will create a great innovation. In music, the more we compose, the more likely it is that one of our compositions will become a masterpiece.

Factor 5: Courage and stubbornness

Innovative people create things not seen before. Therefore, they are likely to be exposed to unjustified or unqualified criticism, discouragement, and ridicule. Consequently, innovative thinking requires courage and stubbornness to ignore impediments. Innovative thinking is a challenging endeavor. Being aware of these factors may help you overcome hindrances.

SYSTEMIC THINKING

There are many complex systems found in all areas of life, including politics, business, finance, technology, nature, and social conduct.

We use systemic thinking when dealing with such complex systems. This type of thinking seeks to understand in great detail how systems work. More specifically, systemic thinking starts with identifying all forms of connectivity, interrelatedness, interfaces, and other important characteristics. This detailed understanding is then used to predict and to assess system responses and outcomes in reaction to our decisions and activities.

In a world of increasing connectivity and rapidly growing systems, systemic thinking is an indispensable tool for proper decision making. However, it is greatly underutilized. Therefore, our decisions and actions may create unintended consequences because of inaccurate or insufficient understanding of how the systems operate.

In Florida, for example, there is a rapidly growing population of invasive animals. One of them is the toxic sugar cane toad. They were brought to the region as a natural and cost-efficient way to deal with insects threatening sugar cane plantations. Decision makers failed to understand how this toad would interact with the environment and its complex systems.

It turned out that the sugar cane toad does not have any natural predator.[37] As a result, the sugar cane toad multiplied and is now found in great numbers in southern Florida, becoming a threat to many native species.

I use systemic thinking on a regular basis as businesses and financial markets operate in extremely complex systems. For example, in early 2000, I led a consulting team that analyzed the stability of the U.S. financial system. We used systemic thinking to map the complex interdependencies and interfaces in the U.S. credit markets. Thanks to systemic thinking, our analysis in 2000 detected the specific weaknesses and deficiencies that would lead to one of the biggest financial crises in U.S. history (the crisis of 2007). It would have been difficult to make these discoveries without using systemic thinking.[38]

STRESS TESTING

Stress testing is an approach to thinking that focuses on finding meaningful mistakes, shortcomings, and insufficiencies. More specifically, stress testing seeks to find faults and unaddressed risks in our thoughts, planning activities, actions, and decision making. It seeks to assess our preparedness for adverse developments and stress scenarios.

Since the financial crisis of 2007, stress testing has been intensively used in the financial industry to detect dangerous vulnerabilities to unaddressed risk exposures. Its usefulness, however, is not limited to the financial world. It should be used in all aspects of life to raise preparedness for adverse developments.

Stress testing sessions focus on all aspects of conduct that could be vulnerable to stress scenarios. More specifically, stress testing activities apply to:

- Our assumptions and beliefs about the present and the future
- All relevant systems with which we interact or on which we rely

- All processes with which we operate, interact, or to which we are exposed
- All routines and common practices
- All solutions, products, and services that we use and offer to others
- All current rules and regulations

Stress testing focuses on finding mistakes, deficiencies, and shortcomings that could expose us to dangerous risks. It helps us to adopt the mindset of a constructive skeptic or detective, eager to secure safety and success.

The technique is little used in our personal lives, even though it could improve our security and success. For example, many U.S. families endured pain and financial losses when they failed to prepare for falling house prices, rising mortgage rates, and the deteriorating economy during the first stage of the financial crisis of 2007. Simple stress testing of a family's financial situation under different stress scenarios (including falling house prices and rising interest rates) would have alerted many families to their financial vulnerabilities. Stress test results would have motivated families to refinance (or change) variable and short-term mortgages, sell down oversized real estate portfolios, or find other ways to reduce their financial leverage.

Companies are well advised to conduct stress tests regularly. Ideally, external consultants facilitate these stress testing activities. Consultants increase the effectiveness of corporate stress tests in multiple ways. They may find issues such as cover up of past mistakes or hidden agendas. Consultants are independent and unbound by political agendas and conflicts and provide expertise in devising stress scenarios.

In our personal life, we should stress test our professional career and marketability, financial stability, and health. We may ask family members and friends to assist us, providing suggestions and assessment of our preparedness.

In conclusion, it is important for critical thinkers to be aware of different approaches to thinking to ensure successful outcomes. Depending on the problem or situation we seek to address, we must use an appropriate thinking tool. Chart 27 introduced a selection of useful thinking tools. Feel free to add others to this selection.

Summary:

In this chapter, the following tools, frameworks, and concepts are discussed:

- *Perspective-based thinking*
- *Consequential thinking*
- *Situational thinking*
- *Strategic thinking*
- *Anticipatory thinking*
- *Innovative thinking*
- *Systemic thinking*
- *Stress testing*
- *Critical observation*

Exercises:

Exercise 1: Use chart 27 to find three situations in your life that would have profited from one of the types of thinking.

Exercise 2: Chose a project you are working on currently (e.g., career move, building/renovating a house, losing weight/becoming healthier). Systematically consider the use of each approach to thinking presented in chart 27 and its potential for helping you achieve better outcomes. The following chart may be used in summarizing your findings.

Chart 32: Exercise Sheet (based on chart 27)

Perspective-Based Thinking	Consequential Thinking
1 _____	1 _____
2 _____	2 _____
3 _____	3 _____
Situational Thinking	**Strategic Thinking**
1 _____	1 _____
2 _____	2 _____
3 _____	3 _____
Anticipatory Thinking	**Innovative Thinking**
1 _____	1 _____
2 _____	2 _____
3 _____	3 _____
Systemic Thinking	**Stress Testing**
1 _____	1 _____
2 _____	2 _____
3 _____	3 _____

EXCURSUS: HOW CRITICAL THINKING IMPACTS YOUR HAPPINESS AND SOCIAL LIFE

Before we move on to the master classes (brown belt here and black belt in the following book), we should consider two important issues to avoid frustration and setbacks when practicing critical thinking:

1. Critical thinking is likely to make you more successful, but this does not mean that you automatically will become happier. The strategies leading to success and happiness do not necessarily overlap. Work needs to be done to gain both success and true happiness.
2. Friction and tension may develop in your social environment when you transition from superficial to critical thinker. Some people will dislike you for challenging their reasoning and analytic rigor, particularly if you were an uncritical follower (before your transition to critical thinking), easy to convince and manipulate.

Both issues may lead to frustration and decreased motivation if unaddressed. The following will help you prepare for these initial difficulties. Targeted action can address and mitigate both issues, requiring proactive strategies and tactics before conflict and frustration arise.

ISSUE #1: CRITICAL THINKING IS LIKELY TO MAKE YOU MORE SUCCESSFUL, BUT THIS DOES NOT MEAN THAT YOU AUTOMATICALLY WILL BECOME HAPPIER.

In my presentations to students, I joke that it is easier to become a millionaire than a truly happy person. There is some truth in this. First of all, becoming a millionaire is a <u>one-dimensional</u> goal: you pick a profession (or skill) in demand and focus on becoming great at it. This can be any profession, sport, or art. As long as you put in long hours and apply critical thinking, you are very likely to succeed. In contrast to previous centuries, modern society is meritocratic, with many different paths to success.

Formerly, birth determined future success. Today, the situation is completely different. Many young people became wealthy by developing their skills in finance, technology, and social media. Facebook alone is probably responsible for hundreds of new young millionaires.

However, not all of these successful people are truly happy. I know many highly successful individuals who have suffered prolonged periods of unhappiness. The reason is simple. Happiness is multidimensional, requiring simultaneous achievement of many different, and sometimes conflicting, goals. These include:

- Good health and safety for you and your family
- Time for family and friends
- Time for relaxation activities and hobbies
- A fulfilling and secure job
- A nice atmosphere at work
- Financial stability

When you start using critical thinking, it is likely that your (professional) success score will grow faster than your happiness score. This is not surprising. The switch from superficial to critical thinking will boost the quality of your analyses and decisions, leading to better outcomes.

Critical thinking and better analyses require much time taken away from activities that support happiness (e.g., time with family and friends). More specifically, on the success path, time is taken from activities that make us happy and spent on activities that make us more successful. This can produce a dangerous downward spiral leading to professional success coupled with increasing unhappiness.

This important thought is explained with the following example (see chart 33).

Chart 33: The connection between success and happiness

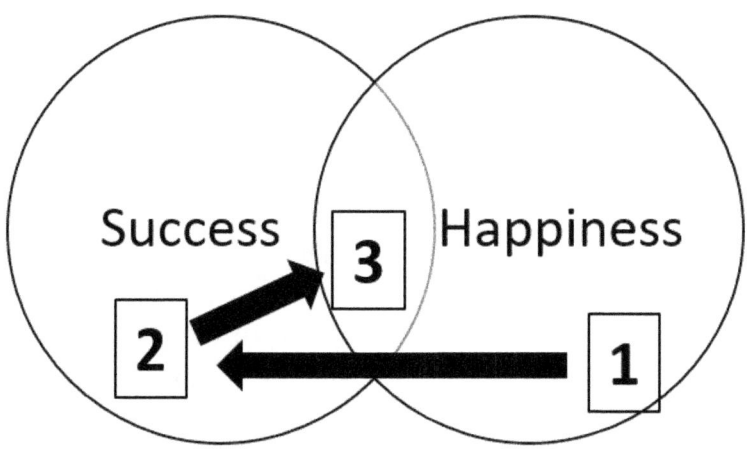

Fictitious case study on success and happiness:

Jason's goal is to become a management consultant with one of the leading consulting firms in New York. He attended an M.B.A. program at a prestigious New England university. The two years Jason spent in university had been wonderful. He enjoyed the subjects he studied, he played soccer for the university team, and he spent a lot of time with his friends. He had been a truly happy person (situation 1 in chart 33). After completing his M.B.A., he was offered a job at a top tier consulting firm in New York. His dedication to critical thinking allows him to perform quite well. Soon, senior partners in the firm referred to him as a black belt in problem solving. The projects he worked on were big successes and the partners promoted him to project leader ahead of schedule.

However, success came at a price. He worked long hours and traveled frequently. He lost touch with his friends and gave up playing soccer. He felt stressed by the workload and responsibility given to him and by the growing expectations of senior managers. He had little time with his girlfriend. In chart 33, he moved from position 1 (happy, not successful yet) to situation 2 (successful, but not happy).

Jason's situation is common in today's professional world. The need for excellent critical thinkers often brings a fast track to success. If not managed proactively, this success may lead to unhappiness and frustration. This becomes the status quo for some people.

My recommendation is to accept situation 2 "successful, but unhappy" for only a brief period of time. The goal is to move on to situation 3, "successful and happy," as soon as possible. Careers and other challenges in life require periods of hard work with limited time for social activities and narrow focus on a single goal. For example, the success of completing a marathon is preceded by a prolonged period of hard, focused training. In my experience, it was not fun to get up on a cold rainy day for a long practice run. A marathon runner has to invest many hours for preparation and practice runs. This means time away from family, friends, and other important activities.

The challenge for critical thinking is to combine success with happiness (situation 3 in chart 33). The use of critical thinking should not be restricted to professional careers only. All important decisions should be based on critical thinking, including the desire for happiness. Therefore, we must use critical thinking to develop strategies that help us move from situation 2 to situation 3.

I have several highly successful friends who accomplished this challenge. They are not willing to compromise their happiness for a prolonged period. One of them explained his philosophy: When you become successful, you gain bargaining power that must be used to exchange some success for happiness. Your company and your boss become dependent on you and your ability to apply critical thinking in problem solving. At this stage, you need to learn to say no to unreasonable workloads and company assignments that conflict with your overall happiness (e.g., business travel that puts stress on you and your family). Remember, once you have become successful, you also have the bargaining power to say no. It is always easier for a critical thinker to find an alternative job that is more suitable for a desired lifestyle than for a company to replace a superb critical thinker.

Critical thinking may also create innovative solutions that help you achieve success and happiness. This includes designing your job to ensure happiness. This is sometimes easier than expected. For example, a consultant who is also an art aficionado may pick projects in cities that offer famous museums, exhibitions, and architecture. Critical thinking skills may provide innovative solutions that increase your efficiency and effectiveness, freeing up time for activities that support happiness.

ISSUE #2: FRICTION AND TENSION MAY DEVELOP IN YOUR SOCIAL ENVIRONMENT WHEN YOU TRANSITION FROM SUPERFICIAL TO CRITICAL THINKER

Social interactions in the modern world are impacted by four powerful forces:

1. Positive thinking: Assuming that things will turn out fine and that there is little reason to worry.
2. Consensus driven decision making: Making compromise decisions to ensure maximum acceptance by everyone involved at the expense of decision quality.
3. Political correctness: The avoidance of any language, statements, decisions, and actions that could (though in some cases accurate) marginalize, insult, single out, or exclude an individual or a group.
4. Inflationary positive feedback: The trend of giving positive feedback even for unsatisfactory performance to avoid uncomfortable situations (i.e., unwillingness to criticize others).

Critical thinking is often not compatible with these four forces and violates at least one of them. For example, adopting an attitude of constructive skepticism may be interpreted as negative thinking, in conflict with the social force of positive thinking. Not surprisingly, black belt critical thinkers often clash with positive thinkers.

It is not the objective of critical thinking to make everyone happy by suggesting that the future is always bright, accepting poor decisions for the sake of consensus or giving positive feedback for poor performance to avoid an uncomfortable situation. Lying creates more harm than good in the long term. Critical thinkers cannot accept such outcomes.

The goal of critical thinking is to seek truth as the basis for better decisions that lead to better outcomes.

Critical thinkers should expect conflict and friction. Therefore, experienced critical thinkers use proactive strategies and tactics to defuse tensions in social environments that include those unfamiliar with the demands of critical thinking.

New critical thinkers may not be aware of this problem and the strategies needed to address it. They are at risk of getting caught in emotional and disruptive discussions that can easily spiral out of control.

It is important that all critical thinkers learn how to implement critical thinking without risking disruption and emotional outbreaks. The key is to use proactive strategies and tactics to defuse conflicts before they become disruptive, dysfunctional, and unmanageable.

The following strategies and tactics help to accomplish this important goal:

- Do not become confrontational during a critical thinking session and avoid using harsh and unnecessarily negative expressions. ("This is totally wrong.")
- Always point out that the debate is not about who is right or wrong, but what is the right decision for the company, team, or family future.
- Never make an issue personal. ("You are always wrong; last time, you were wrong, too.")
- Always make sure that participants understand the consequences of poor or unsatisfactory decisions that are the result of a lack of critical thinking. ("If we get this wrong, our company could get into serious trouble and many of us will lose our jobs.")
- Challenge arguments in a polite and nonconfrontational manner. ("Could you please explain the analysis that backs up your point, as I did not fully understand it. I am particularly interested in your argument XYZ. ")

- When you prove your point after a heated discussion, do not claim victory or celebrate. Instead, try to get everyone back on board and offer praise. ("Thanks to a fabulous team effort, *we* got to a good decision.")

I admire how some business people wrap critical thinking into a smooth conversation. Even though they challenge another's remarks, they never cause them embarrassment. We can learn much from them.

You are likely to experience these situations. With experience and practice, you will master these challenges, but do not underestimate their destructive potential if unaddressed.

Summary:

In this chapter, the following tools, frameworks, and concepts are discussed:

- The connection between success and happiness
- Four powerful forces impacting social interactions and how they suppress critical thinking
- Strategies to defuse heated discussions and avoid confrontation

These exercises use some of the tools, frameworks, and concepts discussed in this chapter:

Exercise 1: Find examples of these among your friends and colleagues (based on chart 33):

    a. Happy but unsuccessful
    b. Successful but unhappy

Use your critical thinking skills to identify strategies and actions that could help them become "successful and truly happy" as outlined in chart 33.

Exercise 2: Find five examples of expert critical thinkers who are successful and happy (coworkers, friends, celebrities). List five lessons learned.

PART II: PREPARING FOR MASTER LEVEL (THE BROWN BELT CLASSES): SUCCESSFULLY DEALING WITH AN INCREASINGLY IRRATIONAL WORLD

CHAPTER 6 - THE BROWN BELT: A CRISIS OF REASONING. HOW AN IRRATIONAL WORLD CHALLENGES CRITICAL THINKERS

This chapter concerns one of the most important issues facing critical thinkers: the crisis of reasoning that surrounds us, or more simply: how does a rational person deal with an increasingly irrational world. A detailed understanding of this issue and its implications is a prerequisite to successful application of critical thinking on an advanced level. Failure to acknowledge the irrationality that often surrounds us and expectation of rational behavior and logical responses to our actions sets us up for disappointment.

Here is an example to introduce the topic. It was reported that the Queen of England once expressed her astonishment that the financial crisis of 2007 was not anticipated by the country's top economists. The reason is simple. Economists, with the exception of those in the new field of behavioral economics, typically base their research on the assumption of rational market participants (e.g., individuals, companies, countries). In a rational world, there are no irrational exaggerations in financial markets leading to bursting bubbles and abrupt disruptions. Therefore, economists' theories and models often fail to explain the real world, particularly prior to the crisis of 2007. Critical thinkers must not replicate this mistake. In this chapter, we learn how to do this and, more specifically, how to incorporate irrationality into the world of critical thinking.

The success of many of our most important decisions is dependent on the responses and behavior of others. If we start our own business, our success depends on how others react to our products and services. We may have the best product in the world that fulfills an important need, but we still may fail. This happens often. In the field of technology, the standard that receives the highest following among customers is rarely the best technological option in the market place, just as the healthiest food options are not the best sellers in restaurants and supermarkets. Observe the content of shopping carts the next time you visit a grocery store. Unhealthy foods typically outweigh healthy choices.

Irrational choices are often the preferred choices. If we assume rational behavior in an irrational environment, our business will not do well (and vice versa).

Unfortunately, the world is more irrational than commonly assumed. When we observe our environment and people's decision-making processes this becomes quite apparent.

For example, most would agree that a healthy, pain-free life is one of our most important goals. Anyone who has suffered illness or pain knows that they can wipe out all happiness and chances for success. Therefore, in a rational world we should pursue only activities that support our health. Most people do exactly the opposite, pursuing choices regarding nutrition, exercise, and health maintenance that sabotage their most important goal (i.e., living a healthy, pain-free life).

Many people are better at protecting the health of their cars (or other less important things) than their own health. They score perfectly at car maintenance (choosing the right gasoline, engine oil, brake fluid) and never miss their annual car tune-up. They would never overinflate tires or drive an overheating engine, but have lower standards when it comes to their health.

In fact, if people maintained their own health as well as their car's health, many health care problems in developed countries would be a thing of the past. Quite an irrational world we are living in!

Not only does the individual behave irrationally, society does as well. To deal with our own irrational lifestyle choices, we create an irrational health care system. In the U.S., little value is placed on preventing illness and disease. Children are often fed unhealthy diets. Unhealthy food choices dominate the shelves in supermarkets. Health insurance places little emphasis on proactive health maintenance and preventive measures.

Another example of widespread irrationality is found in the acceptance of technological innovations. Fifty years ago, the recipient would have objected if the postman delivered a letter that had been opened by an unauthorized person. Today, most of our personal communication is sent in open letters. We call them emails and text messages. Our irrationality does not stop here. An increasing number of people expose their privacy to devices equipped with microphones, video cameras, and recording capabilities not understanding where and how the information is stored and used.

There are many more examples of irrational behavior, but I am sure that the reader gets the point. Now consider how critical thinkers should deal with such irrational behavior.

The good news is that even though irrational behavior is widespread, increasing at an alarming rate, it is not erratic or random. It follows certain patterns and rules that are easily decoded by critical thinkers. Decoding these patterns makes the behavior of both society and individuals more predictable. This enables critical thinkers to anticipate the behavior and responses of others for the development of powerful strategies in business, investments, politics, and social life.

Critical thinkers need to understand the degree of irrationality in their environment and decode the patterns of irrationality that surround them. Here is a selection of five patterns of irrationality that I have observed. There are many more patterns, but the following selection is a good start. The strength of the prevailing pattern may vary in different geographies. Primary and secondary socialization[39] play a huge role in this context.

IRRATIONALITY PATTERN #1: LINEAR EXTRAPOLATION OF THE FUTURE FROM THE RECENT PAST

One of the most common causes of failure is being unprepared for a major risk event. Forming intelligent views of the future and its impact should be a prime activity for individuals and organizations. A systematic, fact-based approach should enable us to anticipate future developments and to prepare for adverse developments. Using critical thinking in this context should enable us to minimize the risk of adverse surprises in our lives.

Unfortunately, society is poor at this task. Most individuals and organizations use naïve and overly simplistic approaches when dealing with future risks and opportunities. Their views of the future are formed by a simple linear extrapolation from the recent past. If times have been good recently, the future is expected to follow this positive trend. If times have been bad, the future is expected to be worse and full of risks. If we have not experienced major risk events in the past decade, we discount the probability of such events in the future. As a consequence, we reduce our attention to risk management matters, often when needed most.

Anyone who has witnessed corporate strategic planning cycles is familiar with this irrationality. Future revenue and profitability targets are not the result of in-depth analyses of the spectrum of future scenarios. Instead, planning goals are set by the trends seen in the previous years. If revenues have increased four and five percent over the past two years, it is likely that the planning goal for the next year will be six percent.

Most risk management tools are based on the same flawed reasoning. Banks, for example, use an approach called "Value at Risk" to assess their exposure to risk events. This approach uses the most recent financial data (typically a period of between one month and one year) to estimate future risk. In other words, events of the recent past are often used to predict risks in the future.

Investment decisions by both professional and personal investors follow the same path. Confidence in positive returns grows if the recent past has been positive. After almost ten years of rising house prices in the U.S., in 2005 few doubted that this trend would not continue. Similarly, during the summer of 2018, after experiencing almost ten years of rising stock markets, most forecasts predicted future stock returns to be positive as well.

Such simple approaches to assessing opportunities and risks may result in negative surprises. Extrapolating the future from the recent past puts risk management at the lowest level of preparedness when it is needed most (i.e., the period before a major swing from good times to bad times).

Knowing this pattern of extrapolating the future from the recent past helps us understand why human behavior is often excessively irrational and allows us to anticipate the build-up of irrational bubbles in investment markets. I have met several successful investment managers whose strategy was to exploit such patterns of irrationality.

IRRATIONALITY PATTERN #2: IN STRESS SITUATIONS, WE FOLLOW OUR PRIMITIVE INSTINCTS THAT LIMIT OUR RESPONSES TO TWO DEFAULT STRATEGIES: FIGHT OR FLIGHT.

Most of us rely on an outdated response repertoire when we encounter stress situations for which we are unprepared, fight or flight. In the past this binary response made total sense (as discussed in previous chapters). When confronted by a wild animal, we could not analyze the best possible response. We needed to act swiftly to survive, making a quick assessment whether to run away or to engage in a fight.[40]

In modern times, these choices tend to be suboptimal for the problems we encounter. We need more sophisticated responses. Today's challenges rarely emerge out of the blue. Even the dramatic changes brought by the internet took years or in some cases decades to materialize. We usually have the time to think, to reflect, to analyze, and to debate well thought out strategic responses. There is no need to restrict our response repertoire to two options, fight or flight. Almost always, we have time to reflect and to think critically before choosing an appropriate response.

Unfortunately, modern life remains dominated by flight or fight responses. Critical reflective thinking is practiced at a diminishing rate. This is true in our personal and professional lives.

This important point is illustrated in this example. The financial crisis of 2007 took most investors by surprise even though it was the result of obvious poor risk management decisions over an extended period of time. When the crisis became apparent, many investors quickly picked the flight strategy and sold their stock holdings. This was the result of instinctive behavior rather than rigorous critical thinking. Falling stock prices created more fear, leading to more investors selling out their stock positions at any price. Stock markets around the globe fell.

Investors who initially chose to fight (e.g., buying more shares) capitulated given collapsing equity markets. They too chose the flight strategy. As the crisis began, the fighters increased their financial positions, convinced that they would win over an (in their view) unjustified nervous market. They fought against falling stock markets, but their strategy was not the result of critical thinking. It was an instinctive action based on a naïve and superficial assessment of the situation, a stubborn view that selling was an act of cowardice.

When both fight and flight groups eventually left the market, stock prices reached irrationally low levels. Most investors, however, refused to buy any stocks as the negative recent past clouded their rationality and they thought that the worst was still to come. They continued on the irrational flight path, thinking it was the safest strategy.

A few investors, however, did not use the outdated fight or flight response. They used critical thinking and reflective reasoning to find countless opportunities to make money. They took advantage of an irrational world. Unsurprisingly, well-known investor Warren Buffett was among those investing in ultra-cheap stocks and offering attractive financing deals. Other investors found relative value opportunities that offered good returns. The investors practicing critical thinking prospered compared to followers of flight or fight.

There are countless examples of fight or flight responses during times of stress. For example, when the Ebola virus first spread outside of Africa in 2014, the overwhelming response was an hysteric adoption of the flight strategy. Media reported that people in cities unaffected by a handful of Ebola cases refused to let their children go to school. When risk events occur, adoption of flight strategies often worsen the outcomes. This is why fire drills are conducted, to prepare for a reflective response to emergencies. Fire drills try to overrule our fight or flight response system. They seek to promote rational over irrational responses.

IRRATIONALITY PATTERN #3: WE ARE OBSESSED WITH GAINING MORE WITHOUT UNDERSTANDING THE DANGER OF AN EVER INCREASING RISK-OPPORTUNITY IMBALANCE.

Any activity we conduct comes with a set of opportunities and risks. In a rational world, we would pursue only activities that promise more opportunities than risks. Rational people would never choose an activity with exposure to excessive risks and uncertainties without being generously compensated. However, this is what we do, sometimes knowingly, sometimes unknowingly.

The reason is that we are living in a *"get more all the time"* society. *Thoughtful moderation* is not what the modern society is about. The *get more all the time society* demands more convenience, more growth, more benefits, more entertainment, and more technological gimmicks from the world we live in. In most cases, we are not particularly interested in the long-term risks that come with the unconditional pursuit of *more*. This is true for both companies and individuals. Both are integral parts of the *get more all the time society*.

One of the motivations for this excessive pursuit of *more* is our inherent bias for assuming that positive outcomes are more likely than negative ones. This is the result of the excessive adoption of positive thinking and our susceptibility to optimism bias. In my view, this phenomenon of positive thinking and positive expectation is rooted in the unparalleled benign living conditions that we have enjoyed over the past fifty years in the developed world (abundance of food, no wars on our territory, no major risk events, continued economic growth, increasing life expectancy). This is in sharp contrast to the general mood during most of history. Experiencing war, recessions, food crises, and many other severe risk events, my parents' generation and their predecessors were not as positive about the future as my generation and today's millennials. In fact, they preferred safety (achieved through thoughtful moderation and proactive risk management) over the pursuit of *more*.

The unconditional pursuit of *more* puts us in a permanent and intensifying risk-opportunity imbalance. Eventually, such excessive and irrational risk taking catches up with us. We have been lucky that risk events of the last fifty years have not created major permanent damage. Over the past fifty years, we always recovered from temporary setbacks and crises. Even the stock market losses during the financial crisis of 2007 have been more than compensated for by the following boom period. Therefore, the compulsion to demand *more* all the time is unbroken. In fact, past recoveries have increased our demand for *more*. This should make us nervous. The *get more all the time society* is on an irrational and dangerous path.

IRRATIONALITY PATTERN #4: WE PREFER SMALL SHORT-TERM REWARDS OVER SUBSTANTIAL LONG-TERM ACHIEVEMENTS.

It is a human fallacy and a pattern of irrationality that most of our decision making fails to balance short- and long-term considerations equally. We focus on the short term, sacrificing better outcomes that could be achieved by anticipating long-term risks.

Companies and investors in the developed world obsess over short-term results. As a consequence, quarterly earnings have become key metrics for management's and investors' decision making. In some cases, companies halt important long-term projects to deliver short-term cost cutting that helps meet quarterly earnings targets.

We see the same short-term versus long term imbalance in lifestyle choices. Food and nutrition choices typically place higher value on short-term pleasure and convenience than on long-term health. Therefore, heart attacks, strokes, type 2 diabetes, and other lifestyle related health risks have increased dramatically.

Short-term thinking is responsible for individuals, companies, and countries not reaching their potentials. As a result, we face mediocre outcomes and are unprepared for major risk events.

It is a pattern of modern society that we forego long-term success and happiness for short-term pleasure and convenience.

IRRATIONALITY PATTERN #5: A STUBBORN RESISTANCE TO GET SMARTER. WE IGNORE INFORMATION AND REFUSE DISCUSSIONS THAT CHALLENGE OUR BELIEFS AND CONVICTIONS (CONFIRMATION BIAS).

One of the most fascinating patterns of irrationality is the so-called confirmation bias, which is the tendency to look for confirmation of our beliefs and hypotheses. It is defined as a "cognitive bias and systematic error of inductive reasoning."[41]

In a rational world, we would test our beliefs and hypotheses, particularly on important topics such as investments and lifestyle choices. We do the opposite. We filter information by eliminating that which challenges our views, beliefs, and decisions.

Socially, we seek out those who confirm our views on business, politics, and investments. This prevents us from gaining new perspectives and insights on emerging opportunities and potential risks.

Confirmation bias is a sign of irrationality. We refuse to improve our analyses and to make better decisions. We do not want to upset our beliefs and convictions, even when they are built on insufficient or false analysis.

Confirmation bias leads to both poor decision making and dangerous risk exposures. It can reinforce herd mentality and groupthink. Unfortunately, it is an effective tool to create more irrationality in today's world.

CONCLUSION

The goal of this chapter is twofold. First, to demonstrate that modern life is increasingly determined by irrational thinking and decision making. Second, and this is the good news, to explain that most of the irrationality that surrounds us is not erratic or unpredictable. Most instances of irrationality follow common patterns. We can study these patterns and use the knowledge we gain to anticipate the consequences of society's irrationality. We can also adjust our critical thinking processes to deal with the irrationality surrounding us.

Knowing the patterns of irrationality enables us to anticipate future developments and outcomes. This gives us a strong competitive advantage in dealing with emerging risks and exploiting future opportunities, the subject of the next chapter. In chapter seven, we discuss strategies that seek to leverage our understanding of the patterns of irrationality. The goal is to develop sound strategies that make us more successful in an irrational world.

Summary:

In this chapter, the following tools, frameworks, and concept are discussed:

- Crisis of reasoning
- Irrationality (how it is widespread in the modern world)
- *Five patterns of irrationality*
    - Linear extrapolation of the present into the future
    - Fight or flight response system
    - The *get more all the time society*
    - Preference for small short-term rewards over substantial long-term achievements
    - Stubborn resistance to get smarter: Confirmation basis
- *Optimism bias*
- *Thoughtful moderation*

Exercises:

Exercise 1: In both your personal and professional lives, find examples of irrational behavior. Study these examples for common patterns of irrationality. Can you find new patterns of irrationality?

Exercise 2: Look back at your own life. What were examples of irrational decision making and behavior that led to suboptimal outcomes? In retrospect, what lessons have you learned from these instances? Note and review the lessons learned.

Exercise 3: Find examples from your experience of the five irrationality patterns discussed.

CHAPTER 7 - THE BROWN BELT: HOW CRITICAL THINKERS CAN TURN WIDESPREAD IRRATIONALITY INTO FORTUNES

The previous chapter describes how and why we are surrounded by widespread irrationality, which leads to suboptimal decisions and poor outcomes. I am not so naïve as to believe that critical thinkers can reduce or eliminate society's irrational behavior in the short term. Moving from an irrational to a rational world requires significant change, targeted analytic work, and disregard of the pursuit of short-term pleasure and convenience. A wide-spread educational effort in critical thinking would be needed to reduce meaningfully the prevalence of irrationality in our society. This is unlikely to happen. Therefore, not only is irrationality here to stay, it is likely to spread even further.

There is, however, good news for critical thinkers. Irrationality is neither erratic nor unpredictable. It systematically follows specific patterns and rules. Knowing these enables a critical thinker to anticipate or even to predict behavior and decisions by both society and individuals. This knowledge creates a broad launch pad for a variety of strategies to exploit this irrationality to our advantage or at least to protect us from the harm inflicted by society's irrationality. Chart 34 presents five strategies for both professional and personal situations. Understanding and applying them is a key to achieving better outcomes in an irrational world. It is also a requirement for gaining your brown belt in critical thinking and moving on to the black belt.

Chart 34: Five strategies to exploit widespread irrationality

Strategy	Description
Outthink competitors (by avoiding irrationality)	Avoid irrationality traps and stick to critical thinking
Surfing the irrationality wave	Take advantage of the momentum created by irrational acting people
Patient Cat	Anticipate what will happen when irrationality subsides and wait patiently for that moment
Leverage collective unpreparedness	Be the best prepared person for an event for which the majority of people failed to prepare
Exploit information asymetry	Gain an advantage by having deeper knowledge about an issue than others

These five basic strategies can protect us from the destructive power of irrationality. They also may help exploit irrationality to our advantage. Many fortunes have been made exploiting society's irrationality. Warren Buffett is a good example of rationally accumulating wealth in an increasingly irrational world.

STRATEGY 1: OUTSMART COMPETITORS (AVOID IRRATIONALITY)

This strategy is both simple and effective. I have witnessed many top managers outperform their competitors with this basic strategy. First, they introduce rigorous procedures and policies to eliminate irrationality from their own companies' conduct. Second, they acknowledge that they are surrounded by irrational behavior, which needs to be reflected in their own rational decision-making processes (assuming rational behavior by others in an irrational world is a sure path to disaster). In other words, they adjust their rationality to the irrationality surrounding them.

Executing these two initiatives in parallel can lead to great success. Let me stress that the success of this strategy lies in the simultaneous application of both. Enforcing rationality in your own environment only creates positive life outcomes if we also acknowledge the irrationality around us and adapt our decisions to it.

For example, successful investors spend significant time on rigorous and rational analyses of potential investment strategies. They also know that the majority of people around them may not engage in such analytical rigor. Instead, they often act quite irrationally (e.g., following the herd). Most people believe that risks diminish with rising share prices and increase their investments as prices rise. This is how financial bubbles emerge. Anticipating such irrationality and knowing when to exit is often the difference between mediocre and great investors. Successful investors are aware of the problem of widespread irrationality in financial markets.

Another example. An experienced management consultant taught me an important lesson at the beginning of my consulting career. I was frustrated that a client was hesitating to adopt our well researched recommendation when he told me that only in mathematics is a straight line the shortest distance between two points. In the real world, getting from point A to B may require many detours. In other words, expecting a client to go straight from the current strategy A to a radically different, but superior strategy B is not realistic. Convincing others to change their strategies or conduct requires patience. Efforts to change are accompanied by setbacks, detours, stubborn resistance, and preference to maintain the status quo. Even the best analysis is unlikely to change this.

Successful business managers and entrepreneurs know this quite well. They know that their customers do not always make rational purchasing decisions and that best-selling products are often not the best in terms of objective criteria such as quality, reliability, and price. Instead, bestselling products are the ones that connect with buyers' preferences. Often, these preferences are quite irrational.

German motorcycle producers fell into this trap of ignoring irrationality. They struggled during the 1980s and 1990s despite their products' superior quality and reliability compared to new Asian competitors. They failed to understand that starting in 1980, young customers were more interested in fancy design and lower initial costs than quality, reliability, and high resale values. Product longevity,[42] reliability, quality, and resale value were not part of young buyers' criteria.

To make good decisions in an irrational world, we must use the two pillars of conduct shown in chart 35.

Chart 35: Two pillars of conduct to deal with irrationality

First Pillar: Relating to our own world	Second Pillar: Relating to the world around us
Unconditional commitment to critical thinking; avoidance of any form of irrationality in our controllable environment	Anticipation of irrational behavior by other people and society (outside of our control), strong focus on detecting the patterns of irrationality and acting accordingly

The first pillar focuses on avoiding irrationality in our controllable environment. Such irrationality can be caused by uncritically following the herd, fashion trends, and unqualified leaders. This requires a strict and unconditional commitment to the principles and requirements of critical thinking. Successful companies have introduced policies and procedures to accomplish this. One is the obligation to dissent regardless of rank when irrational thinking and decision making are detected. The obligation to dissent is a core principle of one of the most successful consulting companies. Not only is it prominently displayed on walls and in employee guides, it is strictly enforced in daily conduct. In this particular company, it is the obligation of a young analyst to dissent with a senior partner when fact-based analysis requires it.

The second pillar of this strategy reminds us not to expect rationality in our environment. We should not assume that others use the same rigorous thought processes as do critical thinkers. Our decisions need to consider and anticipate the likely irrational conduct around us.

During periods of irrational exuberance and unjustified pessimism, rationality is the exception, not the rule. Our decisions must reflect this. It is dangerous to assume rational behavior when irrationality is the norm.

For example, during times of excesses and bubbles in financial markets, we observe widespread irrationality. Whatever well-founded argument we offer, trend-following investors will vehemently dispute and ignore our findings and continue purchasing financial assets valued at excessive (irrational) levels. Our investment decisions must account for this irrational behavior (uncritically extrapolating recent trends into the future). We should not expect rationality to win over irrationality in the short term. Instead, we should be prepared for irrationality to last much longer than rational people may anticipate. Betting against irrationality with put options (short-term instruments that rise in value if underlying stocks fall in value) can be a costly and unsuccessful strategy if irrationality prevails over an extended period.

STRATEGY 2: SURFING THE IRRATIONALITY WAVE

Surfing the irrationality wave is one of the most fascinating strategies in exploiting irrationality. A follower of this strategy can gain great fortune by surfing the momentum wave created by the masses of people who uncritically follow irrational beliefs.

To understand this strategy, look at financial markets. The past decades have been marked by numerous irrationality waves that raised the prices of investment assets beyond rationally justifiable levels. This is how valuation bubbles emerge in financial markets. Most of us recall the emerging markets bubble (late 1990s), internet bubble (early 2000s), the U.S. residential real estate bubble (2007), and the bank stock bubble (2007).[43] All of these have patterns comparable to oceanic waves. They start small and slowly, then accelerate and grow into giant waves. Such irrational waves can last for years in financial markets. Eventually, most of these waves crash with great destructive power.

Irrational momentum waves are caused by remarkable levels of irrational thinking and behavior. While we all know that giant oceanic waves will eventually collapse, we assume the opposite when it comes to irrational momentum waves in financial markets. The bigger the irrational momentum wave, the higher the corresponding confidence among investors that this wave is different[44] and will be long-lasting. Tragically, the highest level of confidence in the stability of the irrational momentum wave is reached just before its spectacular collapse. In other words, a gigantic risk event hits us when we least expect it.

A critical thinker can exploit this pattern by joining the irrational crowd and following its procyclical investment strategies. The critical thinker does so knowing that the financial bubble is based on increasing irrationality and that the wave is likely to collapse spectacularly. One's sole goal is to exploit the upward momentum that is created by a growing irrational herd. We surf on the strengthening wave of irrational behavior. We can call the critical thinker's behavior a form of rational irrationality.

I have come across a number of people who have employed this strategy very successfully. Years before the financial crisis of 2007, I had a conversation with a successful hedge fund manager about financial markets and a risk management project I conducted that received attention in financial media. The conclusion was that the financial world was at substantial risk of a disastrous financial crisis.

Even though the manager completely agreed with my reasoning and my pessimistic conclusions, he still believed that being fully invested in stocks was the best investment strategy. His reasoning was that of a surfer on an irrationality wave. He conceded that real estate markets were ridiculously overvalued and financial markets were excessively leveraged and likely to crash. However, irrationality had not yet peaked; therefore, stocks would climb higher before they crashed. He was perfectly right and his *"surfing on an irrationality wave strategy"* probably made him a rich man.

STRATEGY 3: PATIENT CAT STRATEGY

This strategy is the result of watching the hunting behavior of a neighbor's cat in London. I watched it hunt a mouse in my garden. The mouse successfully retreated to a hole in the wall inaccessible to the cat. The cat seemed to know that the mouse would eventually adopt an irrational strategy and emerge. The cat waited patiently. Only a few minutes later, irrationality set in and the mouse left its safe place – a fatal mistake. The cat waited patiently until the mouse moved away from its safe refuge and then made its decisive move to catch the mouse.

We can employ a similar strategy when exposed to high levels of irrationality. Widespread irrationality always creates opportunities for rational thinkers. We just have to wait patiently for these opportunities to present themselves. We anticipate what will happen when irrationality is replaced by rationality and wait. Critical thinking plays a decisive role in this process.

Irrationality seems to appear in self-reinforcing waves that can last weeks, months, and even years. When these waves approach their peaks, the highest collective conviction is reached. Then it is hard not to follow the irrational crowd. However, this is exactly what the patient cat does. The patient cat anticipates that irrationality waves crash eventually. When this occurs, extremely attractive opportunities may arise for those who did not follow the irrational crowd.

This strategy has worked well for investors such as Warren Buffett. Chart 36 shows the long-term ups and downs of the S&P 500 stock market index in the U.S. using a common valuation tool, price-earnings (PE) ratio.[45] Buffett is known for waiting patiently for good investment opportunities, even when passivity leads to a significant accumulation of uninvested money (cash).

As chart 36 shows, stock markets move in long multiyear waves that alternate between periods of irrational exuberance (extremely high PE ratios meaning high prices for stocks) and periods of irrational fear and risk aversion (extremely low PE ratios meaning low prices for stocks). Over the past one hundred years, stock markets have seen many such waves of irrationality. In my view, stock markets show perfectly how irrationality waves emerge, intensify, and eventually crash. This happens in both directions, leading to stocks oscillating between being extremely expensive and extremely cheap. One may wonder why people do not wait for stocks to become cheap to buy and expensive to sell. This is the patient cat strategy and chart 36 shows that it would have worked well in the past.[46]

Chart 36: S&P 500 *Cyclically Adjusted Price Earnings Ratio* (CAPE) between 1881 and summer 2018[47]

A patient cat simply waits until irrational exuberance and overconfidence collapse and stock prices become irrationally cheap. It is impossible always to pick the lowest point to buy and highest to sell. Just getting close to the absolute lows and peaks presents an attractive strategy. As chart 36 illustrates, history presented numerous opportunities to employ the patient cat strategy successfully. However, only a few did so.

Warren Buffett is one of the best examples of using the patient cat strategy to exploit irrational behavior. He describes his rationale as follows: "Be fearful when others are greedy, and be greedy when others are fearful."[48] This is a good description of the patient cat strategy. When people are irrationally risk averse and shun stock investments due to exaggerated levels of fear (when the PE ratio is very low), expect Buffett to be among the few investors picking up cheap stocks. In the past, Buffett's patience and dedication to rational analysis have been rewarded generously (observe Berkshire Hathaway's performance following crises such as the inflation shock of 1973-1974 and the financial crisis of 2007-2008).

The patient cat strategy is relatively simple and can be used in politics, business, finance, and sports. I know people who employ this strategy in real estate, when buying consumer electronics products (postponing a purchase for six to twelve months after a new product's release can save you a fortune), travel packages, and buying produce at a farmers' market (at the end of the day, discounts can be dramatic). In short, the patient cat strategy can be applied in all aspects of life.

STRATEGY 4: LEVERAGE COLLECTIVE UNPREPAREDNESS

Moderately severe risk events can easily turn into big disasters if not anticipated. Widespread unpreparedness seems to be required for big risk disasters to emerge, such as the 2007 financial crisis. A rather normal price correction in the U.S. residential real estate market (after a decade of rising prices) turned into a global economic crisis, threatening financial and nonfinancial companies in Europe and Asia. The key catalyst for this crisis: widespread unpreparedness. People simply assumed that real estate prices could only go up, an irrational assumption. They were unprepared for an outcome that deviated from their base case scenario.

Collective unpreparedness can initiate a deadly downward spiral of erratic and irrational behavior that subsequently worsens outcomes and creates new problems and risks. This is how big risk catastrophes evolve. People caught unprepared refrain from critical thinking and rigorous analysis, seeking refuge in herd like behavior led by panic and emotional roller coasters.

Such irrational behavior creates opportunities for rational thinkers. In fact, times of collective unpreparedness offer attractive launch pads for successful strategies. While many people lost fortunes in 2007, a small number of investors made great fortunes by being well-prepared. Michael Lewis' book *The Big Short* describes how those few people diligently prepared for a scenario that critical thinkers could have anticipated: a correction of prices of U.S. residential real estate and the massive implications for the banking sector. When few thought such a correction was possible or likely, the investors described in Lewis' book bet on falling house prices and defaulting mortgages. As this was thought to be almost impossible by the majority of market participants, the costs of implementing these investment strategies were quite low.

Situations of collective unpreparedness provide very attractive opportunities for two reasons. First, the entry costs for such strategies (investments or new business ventures) are low as most people think they are unrealistic and unattractive. The price for an "unattractive" asset that is currently not in demand is always low.

Second, when most people realize that they are in a situation of collective unpreparedness, they tend to resort to irrational overreaction. When house prices fell dramatically to irrationally low levels, the same was true for the stock market. Not surprisingly, both markets recovered strongly in the years that followed the crisis.

This strategy is not limited to the financial world. Collective unpreparedness is a universal condition of modern society. When I lived in New York, I often witnessed street vendors selling cheap umbrellas at high prices when people were caught unprepared by a rain shower. A series of sunny days was enough to lower New Yorkers' preparedness for the eventual return of rain showers. Even accurate weather reports did not affect this unpreparedness. As a consequence, price sensitivity for umbrellas collapsed, opening up attractive business opportunities for street vendors.

STRATEGY 5: EXPLOIT INFORMATION ASYMMETRY

Widespread irrationality leads to a substantial level of information (and knowledge) asymmetry. On one side are the relatively few people and organizations that practice critical thinking. They systematically collect all relevant data and information to enable rigorous analyses and thoughtful reflection. Often, relevant information is easily available on the internet. As a consequence, they are well-informed and make better decisions.

On the other side are the many who do not use critical thinking and the analytical rigor that comes with it. They experience a significant information (and knowledge) disadvantage, which leads to poorer decisions and unsatisfactory outcomes.

We find such information asymmetries everywhere. They are the source of many business opportunities and are exploited by the well-informed. Most businesses are built on the premise of exploiting information asymmetry. The bigger the information asymmetry between seller and buyer of a product or service, the bigger the business opportunity.

Due to increasing levels of irrationality and surging preference for superficial thinking and following the herd, the number and size of information asymmetries are growing at an alarming rate. This trend is greatly responsible for the high levels of inequality, both financial and nonfinancial.

Access to good education and discipline (and will) to educate oneself are the key determinants for the degree of information asymmetry in a society. The higher the information asymmetry, the higher the level of financial and nonfinancial inequality.

Theoretically, access to the internet should have lowered the degree of information asymmetry and inequality in society. It has never been easier to access free or inexpensive high-quality education programs, knowledge and information databases, and advice. Often, public libraries offer free access to a wide spectrum of databases. What is missing is the will and discipline to use these programs and databases. It seems that many use the internet and modern technology predominantly for passive entertainment. This unfortunate behavior is another example of widespread irrationality and, tragically, will increase information asymmetry and inequality.

Critical thinkers can leverage information asymmetry into significant competitive advantages, one of the easiest ways of leveraging irrationality to achieve better outcomes.

In the simplest form of this strategy, we initiate targeted actions to improve the current state of information asymmetry whenever we engage in negotiations and transactions. When we buy a car, we first conduct targeted research on the quality of the product, the price negotiation range of the car dealer, and anything else that could improve our bargaining position. The internet can quickly provide us such information.

Any important decision or negotiation should always be preceded by an analysis of how we can improve information asymmetry to our advantage. Doing so should become automatic to any critical thinker.

A WORD OF CAUTION

When dealing with widespread irrationality, there is one strategy that usually ends in disaster: fighting irrationality head-on.

Irrationality is more persistent, stubborn, and lasting than most rational thinkers imagine. It is rarely possible to predict the end of an irrationality wave, be it in financial markets, politics, or society. It is also very difficult to convert irrational people to rationality, particularly if they think that their (irrational) behavior led to their recent gains.

Therefore, any strategy that relies on the exact timing of an irrationality wave is extremely dangerous. Rational thinkers usually tend to underestimate the time needed for irrational thinkers to detect their false assumptions and beliefs. Betting your fortune on a health food venture to profit from a return to healthy eating (a move from irrationality to rationality) may be a losing proposition and a risky strategy (there is a reason why even health food stores carry many "unhealthy" products).

The switch from irrational to rational thinking and behavior often occurs only after a significant trigger event. For example, patients recovering from a heart attack often switch to extremely healthy lifestyle choices. People need such significant trigger events to move from irrationality to rationality.

This chapter offers a selection of five strategies that may be helpful as a starting point when dealing with irrationality in our environment. Please make sure that you understand the <u>respective situational context</u> when crafting a suitable strategy to deal with irrationality. There are many more suitable strategies that focus on this topic. However, the strategies presented in this chapter are a good start to deal with irrationality and possibly turn it into an opportunity.

Summary:

In this chapter, the following tools, frameworks, and concepts are discussed:

- *Five strategies to exploit widespread irrationality*
    - *Outsmart your competitors*
    - *Surf the irrationality wave*
    - *Patient cat*
    - *Leverage collective unpreparedness*
    - *Exploit information asymmetry*
- *Rational irrationality*
- *Irrationality wave*

Exercises:

Exercise 1: Reflect on your experiences with irrationality. Pick at least five situations in which society or people around you behaved irrationally and analyze them.

First, reflect on your own behavior. Did you follow the irrational herd? If yes, why? When did you recognize your own irrational behavior? What caused you to understand your own irrationality?

Second, for each irrational situation, try to analyze which of the five strategies discussed in this chapter would have been an appropriate response. Why?

Exercise 2: Can you find examples of irrational behavior in your current situation (e.g., work, financial markets, real estate market)? Confirm the presence of irrationality and decide if any of these strategies could be used to exploit the irrational situation you have identified.

CHAPTER 8 - THE BROWN BELT: THE POWER OF CRITICAL OBSERVATION

Our ability to systematically observe and rigorously screen our environment for clues and information to help us make better decisions is decreasing at an alarming rate. This is unfortunate as this skill, which I call critical observation, is a powerful tool for becoming more successful. Critical observation provides us with the clues, insights, and relevant information that make our decisions and strategies more successful. It can help us detect risks and opportunities before others do. In fact, most risk catastrophes (such as financial crises, wars, political and social disruptions) are preceded by warning signs and red flags clearly visible to those practicing critical observation.

Critical observation is therefore one of the most important items in the critical thinking toolbox. It is a technique to be mastered before moving on to the black belt classes of critical thinking. Critical observation forces us to look at reality systematically with great focus before making important decisions. This reality check helps us to unmask myths, false ideas and beliefs, wrong assessments, and unjustified claims that could contribute to poor decision making.

Being a critical observer of reality differentiates us from those who base their decisions on superficial, incomplete, or incorrect observations. An experienced critical observer can gain three distinctive advantages:

- Reality becomes less complex and less opaque,
- Life outcomes and the forces that determine them become more understandable and more predictable,
- Being caught unprepared by adverse surprises becomes less likely.

Critical observation focuses on four groups of insights:

1. Meaningful patterns and anomalies,
2. Relevant correlations, interdependencies, and potential causalities,

3. New or previously undetected trends and changes in our environment and, more generally,
4. New information on relevant issues.

Critical observation has played a decisive role in many medical breakthroughs, technological innovations, and business and investment successes. It not only increases the effectiveness of critical thinking, it also advances analysis to decision making.

Unfortunately, the tool of critical observation is not used commonly. Most of us are in a state of reduced awareness and partial blindness. Constant distraction by phones, internet, social media, television, and other diversions, as well as our passivity and cognitive laziness, results in our missing relevant information that could help us understand reality and make better decisions. We are trapped in a world of superficial observation and distraction leading to a false, biased, and incomplete understanding of reality.

Quick exercise to test our awareness and alertness:

Test 1:

Think back to the last three business meetings you attended. Describe the mood of each person when the meeting ended; if it was a large group, name three people who seemed unhappy at the end of the meeting. [49]

Test 2:

Can you remember the full names and professional backgrounds of the last twenty people whom you met?

Most people cannot complete these exercises. They are too distracted to pay attention to people or to remember their names and professional backgrounds. This is in sharp contrast to highly successful people. They are alert, screening their environment for new information that could give them a competitive edge. For example, one successful top manager carries always a little Dictaphone in his pocket to record immediately any relevant observation. He carefully archived observations for later reference. His radar is always on. He does not miss an important observation.

Most people miss out on the advantages of critical observation. They ignore the many sources of information around them that could improve their decision making. Superficial observation leads to serious negative consequences:

- We fail to detect valuable clues, information, and insights that could improve our understanding of reality and could result in better decision making.
- We fail to anticipate risks and opportunities.
- Our unawareness and misunderstanding of reality expose us to dangerous levels of unpreparedness and vulnerability.
- We can easily be manipulated by others.

> **Real world example:**
>
> *I often witness young professionals in giving business presentations. The most common mistake they make is not observing the audience. This lack of critical observation often endangers the success of their work. They fail to detect highly important information: Do the listeners understand the points I make? Do they agree? Do the top decision makers in the audience agree? Should I slow down and repeat a crucial argument? Is the audience bored; should I move faster? The best content does not help if the audience disagrees with the main points or simply does not understand the key messages. Critical observation of the audience helps to keep a high level of engagement.*

To avoid the negative consequences of superficial observation of our environments, we must develop and train our critical observation skills. Here is a practice example that addresses a common problem: how to lose weight and live a healthier life. For me, critical thinking played a decisive role in tackling this problem.

In 2010, a routine checkup encouraged me to tackle two issues: losing weight and rectifying some negative health parameters. While my overall state of health was good, I decided that actions had to be taken to avoid more serious problems in the future.

If you want to lose weight and improve your health, you easily find yourself in a confusing and frustrating situation. When you type "healthy living" into the search box of Amazon books, you receive more than 60,000 responses.[50] There are many medications and supplements to help you achieve certain goals. But the frustration and confusion does not stop here. The recommendations given by health experts are often contradictory and change over time. Therefore, it is not surprising that many people fail to achieve their health and weight loss goals simply because they are confused by a cacophony of contradictory information and recommendations.

I decided to create my own health program based on critical observation of reality. There are many people around me who are busy but managed to stay lean and healthy. My hypothesis was that I have to study these positive role models and learn (with some adjustments) from their strategies and habits. Obviously, I would use critical thinking to double-check the validity of my observations and conclusions.

I focused on three core activities:

- Use critical observation to identify positive and negative role models and study their habits and behavior in great detail (i.e., eating preferences and habits, exercise behavior, speed, frequency, and timing of eating). In other words, I started doing my own research based on my own observations of reality.
- Based on these critical observations, I built hypotheses to explain the difference between positive and negative role models. More specifically, I tried to find concrete differences between healthy and unhealthy people that explain the different outcomes.
- Observe the situational context that may impact the behavior and outcomes of studied individuals.[51]

Critical observation needs to be diligent and thorough. The more focused the observation, the more valuable the results. My observations of positive and negative role models were gathered using a wide spectrum of observation activities (see chart 37).

Chart 37: Employing *Critical Observation* to identify healthier lifestyle choices – Illustrative case example

Selection of activities
• Analyze case studies of the elderly. What differentiates positive and negative role models? A special focus was given to those older people who were particularly vital, energetic, healthy, and mentally sharp. I found them among family members, colleagues, friends, and biographies of famous people.[52] • Scrutinize the shopping carts in grocery stores of people who appear to be positive or negative role models. What are the key differences? • Observe the behavior of colleagues at work (snacking behavior, what/how much they ate at business dinners, do they have dessert? How fast do they eat?). • Find turnabout examples (people who significantly improved their overall health: what were the key changes in their lives). • What do successful, healthy top managers eat? What are their lifestyle choices?[53]

I was astonished by how quickly I identified significant behavioral differences between the positive and negative role models. Success or failure did not seem to be accidental. A critical observer could easily find different lifestyle and nutrition choices between the two groups. I also noticed that positive role models were not only healthier. They were more energetic, less moody, happier, and more successful. This observation created additional motivation for me to change my nutrition and lifestyle choices dramatically.

I summarized my observations and conclusions in a personalized health program[54] that was tailored to my goals, needs, and restrictions. The results were impressive. Not only did I achieve all of my health goals, I surpassed many of my goals by a wide margin.

Critical observation can be applied in all aspects of life. We know famous fictional detectives, such as Sherlock Holmes and Colombo, who used critical observation to find the decisive clues to solve complex criminal cases. Often, these decisive clues were not seen by the superficial observer. Critical observation was required to detect them.

Many famous scientists, military leaders, business people, and investors owe their success to their ability to conduct critical observation. Many breakthroughs in science, technology, and business were achieved through critical observation (see chart 38).

Chart 38: Breakthroughs enabled by *Critical Observation*

Major science/innovation breakthroughs made possible by *Critical Observation*
- Alexander Fleming: Observed that accidental mold build-up in an experiment killed bacteria and went on to develop penicillin. - Isaac Newton: Understood gravity by observing an apple falling from a tree. - Konrad Lorenz: Detected behavioral and social patterns by critically observing nature and in particular graylag geese. He was awarded the Nobel Prize in 1973. - Darwin: Developed theory of evolution based on critical observations of nature. - George de Mestral: Observed seeds stuck to his clothes on a hunting trip, using a reversible hook and loop system. This observation led to the development of the Velcro fastening system.

The discovery of penicillin by Scottish scientist Alexander Fleming is interesting, as it shows that critical observation can lead to accidental discoveries. Returning to his laboratory from vacation, Fleming realized that fungus grew in one of his experimental cultures. He probably had failed to close the container properly before he left the laboratory. Many would have thrown the contaminated container in the trash, but Fleming took a closer look and made an historic observation. He realized that the staphylococci bacteria close to the fungus died, while the bacteria farther away from the mold survived. This observation led to the development of penicillin, a powerful antibiotic that has saved millions of lives.[55]

Austrian Nobel Prize winner Konrad Lorenz used critical observation as a core research tool. Lorenz studied behavioral aspects of humans and animals. He became famous for his work observing the behavior of graylag geese and detecting several forms of instinctive behavior. For example, his observations showed that young graylag geese bond with the first moving object they sense after hatching whether this object was the mother goose or a human.

Lorenz' discoveries could not have been made by any other research method at that time. Only focused critical observation allowed him to decode human and animal behavior.

George de Mestral is another great example of the power of critical observation. Others brushed seeds off their clothes after walking through bushes in a forest; de Mestral, however, did not. He was curious why some seeds could stick so effectively to his clothes and dog but were easy to remove by hand. Using a microscope, he discovered a powerful natural hook and loop system. This observation led to the invention of the Velcro fastening system, which made de Mestral famous.

Critical observation, whether conducted purposefully (Lorenz) or not (Fleming), is often the decisive steppingstone to success. We should recognize this and limit the distractions that blur our understanding of the world. The following suggestions may help you build your critical observation skills.

HOW TO GET STARTED WITH CRITICAL OBSERVATION

For many of us caught in a world of superficial observation, it may be difficult to switch to a more active, alert, and focused way of observation. Time and patience are required. Chart 39 lists some of the requirements for successful critical observation.

Chart 39: Requirements for successful *Critical Observation*

Critical Observation: getting started	
<ul><li>Curiosity</li><li>Patience/time</li><li>Open-mindedness</li><li>Willingness to ask questions/formulate hypotheses</li><li>Observe objects and situations from varying perspectives</li><li>Constant cycle of observing, hypotheses building, testing, and refining hypotheses</li></ul>	<ul><li>Courage to challenge status quo</li><li>Constructive skepticism</li><li>Training in pattern recognition</li><li>Constant radar screening of our environment for material clues</li><li>Alternate between macroscopic and microscopic observation</li></ul>

A change in perspective is important to the practice of critical observation. This includes looking at an issue from different angles, alternating between a microscopic view (detailed focusing on a small area) and a macroscopic view (looking at the bigger picture). Switching from a microscopic to a macroscopic perspective may lead to deeper insights into how things work.

The following chart provides a framework for organizing and directing critical observation projects.

Chart 40: Organizing our *Critical Observation* activities

Activity	**Goal**
Screen	• 360-degree screening of environment to gather relevant information
Detect	• Patterns, trends, causalities, interdependencies, correlations
Compare	• Compare sample observations with those from the past, different locations and societies
Challenge and Question	• Challenge status quo and conventional wisdom • Explore alternative explanations
Conclude	• Build new hypotheses based on insights gained

Critical observation has helped me gain important insights into how things work. For example, it helped me succeed professionally in different countries, cultures, industries, and circumstances. The insights generated by critical observations were the foundation of many important decisions in my personal and professional lives.

As a management consultant, critical observation enabled me to:

- Identify dangerous risks and attractive opportunities
- Identify opportunities for operational improvements for my clients
- Identify and anticipate new trends, disruptions, and developments more quickly
- Gain new insights that resulted in a change in strategy, tactics, or behavior

As a result, I was able to build a track record that helped me gain the trust of my clients. It also improved anticipation of challenges and threats to prepare my clients appropriately. In this context, I developed a new approach for my clients: *future anticipation*. It uses critical observation and critical thinking to identify forces and trends that will shape future outcomes. Systematically identifying a wide range of possible future scenarios (and preparing proactively for their impact on us) greatly reduces the chances of being caught unprepared. In fact, doing so often creates a valuable and sustainable competitive advantage over a company's competition.

The following example illustrates the concept of future anticipation using both critical observation and critical thinking.

Real world case example: how critical observation helped me anticipate the financial crisis of 2007

In late 1999, I observed activities in the U.S. credit markets that made me curious. I was working as a management consultant in New York and developed a particular interest in risk management topics. The following critical observations raised some questions for me:

- While U.S. indebtedness reached record levels, it was getting easier to get credit (loans and mortgages). Some banks advertised that they would approve your loan "while you wait."
- Banks entertained the idea of drastically downsizing credit risk management staff as they felt less need to analyze credit risk.
- Banks' incentive systems strongly encouraged employees to originate new mortgages and loans (with less effort on analyzing credit risk). This happened in the context of new bank strategies that focused on repackaging and trading credit risk rather than keeping it (a technique also known as securitization).
- My mailbox was flooded with preapproved mortgage and credit card advertisements. This was just a few years after having experienced problems getting approved for a credit card (due to not having credit history in the U.S.).

- Friends moving to Manhattan told me that they bought an apartment (facilitated by a large mortgage) instead of renting one, as renting was too expensive.

These observations did not make sense. I knew from my experience in risk management that credit risk is a so-called long tail risk. Loans made in good times can easily default during bad times (many years after the origination of the loan). Therefore, to treat credit risk as a short-term risk creates a future problem.

I initiated a research project to analyze the long-term stability of the U.S. banking and credit markets. This project confirmed my initial hypotheses as it identified serious deficiencies in the way credit risk was measured and managed in the U.S.

These deficiencies created substantial and sometimes hidden credit risks that could lead to massive losses in the long term. In fact, the results of my research project suggested that a severe financial crisis was likely if these deficiencies remained unaddressed, leading to poorly managed credit risks. In other words, it was only a question of time until the banking system would experience a severe crisis.

Unfortunately, instead of addressing the issues identified, financial institutions accelerated their efforts to originate and repackage credit risk in the years following my research. While benign market conditions helped for a few years, the U.S. financial system was eventually hit by a severe crisis in 2007. Due to my dedication to critical observation, I was able to raise this issue with many clients long before the crisis.

Critical observation helped me anticipate the financial crisis of 2007 and warn clients to prepare for it. It was a good example of the use of critical observation to anticipate potential risks.

Therefore, I highly encourage learning and practicing this skill. You can do it alone, with a friend, or with a group. A group may provide additional benefits as people make different observations.

Summary:

In this chapter, the following tools, frameworks, and concepts are discussed:

- Critical observation
- Future anticipation
- Framework for organizing our critical observation projects (screen, detect, compare, challenge and question, conclude)

Exercises:

There are many ways to practice critical observation. The following examples are not just practice exercises. They can generate insights that may directly affect your success in your professional and personal lives. I also encourage you to create your own exercises to practice this important skill. You may do so alone, with a partner, or with a group.

1. Pick five positive and five negative role models for a certain subject (professional career, health, sports). Use critical observation to identify why each person is assigned to a group. What are common behavioral traits of those in each group? What can you learn from them to become more successful?
2. Pick two to five successful people in your company (or in your community) who have been significantly more successful than you. Practice critical observation to identify all differences between your daily conduct and theirs. Do not evaluate the differences, make a laundry list. From this list, form hypotheses on why those people may have been more successful than you. Prioritize your observations. What are the top five to ten things you could learn from them?
3. Critically observe your surroundings and identify new trends, products, and ideas worth investment. Identify new trends among certain age groups (fashion, book topics, behavior). Identify examples of unsolved problems that create frustration. Then use your observations to create business ideas to capitalize on the new trends, products, and unsolved problems.

4. On a family excursion, play the following game. Everyone secretly takes five photos featuring objects that they believe the others have not noticed. Then everyone presents the photos and the others guess where they were taken and what they show.
5. The next time you watch your favorite sports team, pretend that you are an external consultant whose job is to suggest new ideas and strategies to make the team more successful. Watch your team and their competitors as a critical observer (not a passive spectator) to identify problems, issues, and improvement opportunities. Then, develop a set of recommendations for the head coach. The goal is to change from being a passive, superficial observer to an active critical observer (even while watching sports).

PART III: A LOOK AHEAD TO THE BLACKBELT CLASSES AND NEXT STEPS

CHAPTER 9: LOOKING AHEAD TO BLACK BELT CLASSES

Becoming a master level critical thinker requires continued learning, questioning, and practice, which is likely to lead to success. The goal of this book is to give you a good foundation in critical thinking. For many of you, this is a significant change in the way you approach problems, interact with others, and make important decisions. The ideas, concepts, tools, and real world examples will help you become a solid critical thinker.

The next book will move you to the master level: the black belt classes of critical thinking. *Success through Critical Thinking Part II*[56] discusses a wide spectrum of topics that will advance you to the master level of critical thinking.

This chapter offers a preview of some of the concepts, issues, and topics discussed in the black belt classes (i.e., the second book in this series). I offer this preview for two reasons. First, to motivate you to continue your journey to becoming a critical thinker. There are still many exciting topics to be explored. Second, to highlight the importance of lifelong learning. There is always a need and an opportunity for improvement. We will always have new learning experiences that open up new opportunities for a successful life. This is particularly true in a complex, fast changing world. A selection of issues, concepts, and ideas discussed in the next book are presented here.

Critical thinkers need to learn how to deal with social complications, particularly when they encounter supervisors, colleagues, and others who are the opposite of true critical thinkers. Every day, at work and in our personal lives, we are exposed to abrasive, short-tempered, confrontational, opinionated, and superficial people. The same way a martial arts practitioner has to learn to fight with unfair and difficult opponents, a black belt critical thinker needs to learn how to deal effectively with difficult and dysfunctional people.

The black belt classes devote particular attention to this problem in the chapter *"How to deal with difficult people – The battle between the LOST (Loud Obnoxious Superficial Thinkers) and the SOUND (Soft-spoken Uncertain Nonconfrontational Deep Thinkers).* [57]

Early in my professional career, I made an important discovery about life in general, and corporate life in particular. There are two extreme types of people: the *LOSTs* and the *SOUNDs*. The *LOSTs'* main goal is dominance in every situation. They are often poor at critical thinking. Their style is abrasive and confrontational, spreading fear and demanding obedience.

LOSTs can bring down teams, organizations, and countries if they are in leadership positions and allowed to multiply throughout a social system. *LOSTs* are a serious threat to the long-term success of an organization or team. They do better for themselves than for their organization.

SOUNDs represent hope. They are reflective and think before they speak. They insist on in-depth analysis and constructive debate before reaching a conclusion. Because of this insistence on doing the analytical work before making material decisions, they may be undeservedly labeled as slow, difficult, and indecisive in the corporate world. A true *SOUND*, however, is a powerful black belt in critical thinking and creates enormous value to any organization that provides the platform and culture for a *SOUND* to bloom.

Unfortunately, *SOUNDs* often lack the firepower, political wit, and general know-how to sell their ideas effectively. They are the hidden gems in average or poorly performing organizations.

In the black belt classes, we learn how to deal with the *LOSTs* and how to limit the damage they inflict. We also look into the creation of a culture that encourages *SOUNDs*. We then consider how *LOSTs* and *SOUNDs* can work together symbiotically and create value to an organization.

The examples of *LOSTs* and *SOUNDs* highlight the social problems that critical thinkers may encounter. But there are many more facets of critical thinking that need to be examined in the black belt classes. Additional chapters taken from *Success through Critical Thinking – Part 2* are highlighted:

A POWERFUL SUCCESS BOOSTER: THE COMBINATION OF CRITICAL THINKING AND RISK MANAGEMENT OR ACHIEVE MORE IN LIFE WITH LESS RISK

This chapter provides an intelligent (and not an emotional) approach to managing the risks in our lives. Advanced knowledge in risk management is indispensable to becoming successful, and also important to remaining successful. Too often, we witness successful individuals, teams, and organizations experiencing significant failures. In most cases, such "boom-bust" incidences are the result of poor risk management practices. A single risk event for which an individual or organization fails to prepare may be enough to wipe out all prior successes. Therefore, risk management is of highest importance for becoming and remaining successful.

Risk management is nothing more than applying advanced critical thinking to the identification, analysis, and management of risks (and opportunities). The goal is not a total avoidance or elimination of risks. Progress and success require taking risks. However, we need to manage carefully the balance of risks and opportunities.

Critical thinking is an important tool for achieving more while taking fewer risks. You may call this a free lunch (achieve more with less risk). For example, the goal of a mountain climber is not to stay at home to avoid the risk of a fall. It is to reach the top of challenging mountains while lowering risk exposure to acceptable levels through proactive risk management strategies. He does so by applying critical thinking to his risk management efforts.

In many situations, the use of critical thinking in risk management enables us not only to contain or limit our risk exposure, but also to turn risks into opportunities. Warren Buffett continues to be a good example of someone who repeatedly turns risk events (e.g., financial crises) into attractive opportunities. A large number of his most successful investments result from severe risk events.

The black belt classes of critical thinking also cover many of the fascinating paradoxes that are part of risk management, such as accurately differentiating risks and opportunities. Often, a perceived risk turns out to be an exceptional opportunity (et vice versa). We may perceive situations as opportunities that are actually dangerous risks. Prior to the financial crisis of 2007, many investors believed that debt leveraged investments in U.S. residential real estate were attractive opportunities. Later, these turned out to be dangerous risks. We learn in the black belt classes that our perception of reality is often misleading. It can be incomplete, biased, or just wrong. Inaccurate or false perceptions of reality expose us to dangerous risks. It is important to be aware of these limitations of perception and to learn how critical thinking can help overcome them.

UNDERSTANDING THE IMPORTANCE OF PERSPECTIVE: THE DIFFERENCE BETWEEN A MACROSCOPE AND A MICROSCOPE

In addition to risk management and reality perception issues, the black belt classes also study the issue of varying perspectives. When we look at an object, issue, or situation, we generally adopt two fundamentally different perspectives. We can take a microscopic view that cuts out the big picture and focuses in great detail on a small segment of a situation or object. This is a common approach in analyses and problem solving. A microscope helps a scientist to see details that otherwise would be undetectable. Microscopic analyses are also common in politics, business, law, and many other disciplines.

A microscopic analysis often may not be sufficient to get to the best decision. It may lead to wrong conclusions. Complex systems that have a high degree of connectivity among system elements and interfaces cannot be studied solely by using a microscope. Another tool that is the opposite of a microscope is needed: a macroscope.

Macroscopes and macroscopic analyses have been widely neglected. We simplify reality by ignoring the many common connective and interrelated issues. As a result, many of our important decisions are false, leading to grave consequences, often with a significant time delay.

A macroscope provides a holistic and wide-angle perspective of an object or situation. It helps detect interdependencies, connective issues, correlations, trends, and relevant patterns. Macroscopic analyses are essential when dealing with complex financial, economic, social, political, environmental, and living systems.

Choosing the right perspective is important to good decisions and positive outcomes. A dentist performing a complex tooth restoration needs to adopt a microscopic focus. The dentist will focus on one area only.

However, when a doctor has a patient experiencing unexplainable pain, it is necessary to combine microscopic and macroscopic analyses. The doctor considers a wide spectrum of possible causes before focusing on a particular hypothesis. Similarly, politicians seeking to reform complex systems such as health care and insurance should use macroscopic analyses.

The black belt classes spend significant time on how to conduct effective and efficient macroscopic analyses and combine them with other approaches (e.g., microscopic analysis).

THE DANGER OF POSITIVE THINKING: HAPPY LOSERS AND WORRIED OVERACHIEVERS

Positive thinking is incompatible with critical thinking. Positive thinking and critical thinking are opposing ends of a continuum.

Positive thinking encourages expectation of positive outcomes. Worrying about life's uncertainties and challenges is actively discouraged. Positive thinking leads in the short term to feelings of euphoria, confidence, and happiness, even though no measurable improvement has been achieved. This may explain the enormous popularity of the concept.

In the long term, positive thinking exposes us to risks of failure and losses because it is based on a biased view of reality and future outcomes. Entertaining unjustified positive expectations of the future can have disastrous consequences:

- A chronic tendency of being unprepared for adverse future outcomes (e.g., risks, negative disruptions of the status quo, trend reversals),
- An inclination to underperform in competitive or challenging situations due to expectation of positive outcomes,
- Frustration and depression due to failure to achieve ambitious goals and disappointment over failure to meet our positive expectations.

The black belt classes devote a chapter to the challenges created by an excessive use of positive thinking in the modern world. My criticism of positive thinking should not be interpreted as an endorsement of negative thinking and pessimism. Negative thinking suffers from the same systematic misperception of reality as positive thinking. Pronounced negative thinking rarely leads to good outcomes and is more likely to produce lethargy, depression, and paralysis.

The black belt classes explain how critical thinking avoids the shortcomings of such biased approaches (positive thinking) to achieve superior outcomes. More specifically, why critical does not mean negative (a common criticism brought forward by positive thinkers) is discussed. In fact, being critical is something extremely positive as it increases our chances for a more successful life.

THE INTELLIGENCE TRAP: THE PROBLEM OF BEING INTELLIGENT ENOUGH TO CHANGE THE WORLD, BUT NOT INTELLIGENT ENOUGH TO MAKE IT BETTER

Human society is without question intelligent enough to make substantial and often permanent changes to the planet and its most vital systems. There is doubt that we are intelligent enough to ensure that these changes are for the better. Issues such as environmental pollution may support the hypothesis that human society is on course to self-destruct due to high, but eventually insufficient, intelligence.

Critical thinkers run into similar problems. The ability to change the world seduces people not to consider long-term consequences or *low frequency but high severity risks*. Individual and collective intelligence may be too limited to interfere successfully with the complex systems of the world, particularly if we take a long time to judge the outcomes of our actions.

There are many examples that support the hypothesis of insufficient intelligence for successful material interventions, innovations, and modifications in complex physical and social systems. For example, we enjoy record levels of human longevity. While we assume that longevity will continue, we greatly interfere with the complex systems that brought us longevity: natural food production, environmental protection, social harmony, and education (to name a few). As a result, children and young adults struggle with serious health issues of epic proportions compared to previous generations (e.g., obesity, allergies, type 2 diabetes, high blood pressure, impaired mental health). Changes that we made to crucial systems have led to severe negative consequences. In many cases, decision makers are not even aware of these developments.

The key question is: Are we intelligent enough to change and interfere with complex systems without risking serious long-term damage? Should we limit our innovative creativity or create circuit breakers to postpone material changes until we have a better understanding of the long-term consequences? Should we avoid interfering with complex systems, or even avoid the creation of such highly complex systems?

These are important questions for critical thinkers. We discuss these issues and possible solutions in the black belt classes.

HOW REAL IS REALITY? IS OUR PERCEPTION OF REALITY ACCURATE OR JUST AN ILLUSION? HOW CAN WE RESIST THE ATTEMPTS BY OTHERS TO MANIPULATE OUR PERCEPTION OF REALITY?

I cannot count the instances in my life when my perception of reality was not in sync with the real world. As a result, I have made poor decisions and have no doubt that I will continue to do so in the future. Most people have had similar experiences. Understanding reality is difficult, particularly when it comes to the social world and its interdependencies, connectivity, and reflexivity.

Our poor track record of perceiving reality is the result of several factors. Critical thinkers must recognize these factors to avoid misperceptions that could lead to poor decision making and suboptimal outcomes. Factors that lead to false perception of reality may include the following situations:

- Manipulation by others (e.g., media, opinion leaders, friends),
- Incomplete, superficial, or false analysis,
- Lack of critical life experience that prevents correct assessment of reality,
- Unknown exposure to systematic biases that lead to misperception (e.g., being an optimist or pessimist),

- A track record of success that encourages overconfidence and complacency leading to decision making without proper analyses,
- An "addiction" to positive thinking that may lead to a constructed view of reality that fits our positive expectations,
- Any form of distraction or misinformation.

Often, primary or secondary socialization may explain the origin of perception issues. In other words, our upbringing greatly influences how we view the world.

Being alert to such issues is extremely important. The critical thinking tool kit offers many concepts and tools to improve the accuracy of our perception of reality. In the black belt classes, this is discussed in great detail.

BEING NORMAL DOES NOT MEAN BEING RIGHT OR WHY CRITICAL THINKERS SHOULD NOT AIM TO BE NORMAL

Critical thinkers know that normalcy is a tricky concept. What is considered normal is not derived from an objective analytical process, but is often the result of a majority vote among the members of a social group. Being normal does not necessarily mean being right. Depending on the distribution of intelligence within a social group, normalcy can have a high probability of being wrong about important things or of not fully exploiting our potential. Therefore, trying to be normal may not lead to better life outcomes or more happiness.

For example, what is now considered a normal diet is often suboptimal at best. It may consist of highly processed or industrialized food, excessive amounts of salt and sugar, questionable chemicals, and lack of fruits and vegetables.

Being normal not only prevents critical thinking, it may also limit potential success.

Critical thinkers should note that the definition of normal changes. One hundred years ago, interfaith marriages were not normal in Europe. Today, however, such marriages are a normal occurrences.

Critical thinkers often clash with the requirements of normalcy. In some cases, they are criticized or singled out for not being normal. When I decided to make healthier lifestyle choices, I ran into this problem. Simply eliminating added sugar from my diet made me "not normal" and subjected me to intense questioning by "normal" people.

Critical thinkers need to be aware of this issue and learn how to deal with frictions that result from deviating from the current definition of normalcy. *Normal people* are often uncritical thinkers who are not (yet) open minded enough to engage in rigorous analyses that question their beliefs, routines, and traditions. In such cases, it is helpful to defuse discussions and avoid emotional outbursts. The black belt classes propose strategies to deal with the issues that emerge when *normal people* reject critical thinking and challenge its results.

WHY CRITICAL THINKERS SHOULD VIEW MISTAKES AS OPPORTUNITIES AND NOT AS FAILURES

Mistakes are often not easily forgiven. Chances are high that an employee will be dismissed after a single consequential mistake. Society is obsessed with punishing mistakes. Do not expect forgiveness or empathy if you commit a mistake in a political or corporate environment. Be prepared for possibly excessive punishment.

Treating mistakes as punishable events can have serious negative consequences, such as:

- Encouraging defensive behavior that denies mistakes (instead of admitting being wrong, fixing the damage, and learning from it),

- Covering up or hiding mistakes instead of rectifying and containing the damage caused by the mistake,
- Failing to draw valuable learning experiences from the analyses of mistakes (e.g., organizational and individual learning),
- Increasing the likelihood of repeating the same mistakes.

Failing to treat mistakes as valuable learning experiences significantly limits the success potential of individuals, teams, and organizations. It is essential to have a policy for handling mistakes. Critical thinking processes must encourage the admission of mistakes and errors. Hiding, debating, or politicizing mistakes is dysfunctional behavior that cannot be tolerated by critical thinkers.

Best practice processes for handling mistakes need to address a wide range of issues. First, it is important to uncover and fully understand a mistake and its possible consequences. Without assessing blame, all efforts should be made to rectify the mistake and limit negative consequences. Second, and this is enormously important for instilling a culture of critical thinking, the thought processes that led to the mistake need to be analyzed to avoid repetition. Mistakes should lead to an open-minded review of thought processes that led to the mistake. History is full of examples of financial crises that are all linked to the same faulty thought processes and mistakes. Unfortunately, instead of learning from those mistakes we continue to repeat them. Third, the lessons learned from analyses of mistakes need to be documented and archived. This archive should be open to all members of an organization for review and learning.[58]

The black belt classes of critical thinking discuss in detail how individuals and organizations can adopt a meaningful approach to handling mistakes.

INTUITION AND CRITICAL THINKING: ARE YOU NUTS TO FOLLOW YOUR GUTS?

Critical thinkers are often confronted with the claim that gut instinct may be better than critical thinking. Senior investment managers frequently run into this problem when less experienced traders want to execute a trade based not on rigorous and sufficient analysis, but on gut feeling or intuition. Often, less experienced traders demand: "Let me do this trade, I know it is going to be a winner." A senior investment executive (and black belt critical thinker) told me that such initiatives set off alarm bells. Some gut feeling trades may turn out to be profitable. Such outcomes are often the result of big numbers in statistics and not proof of intuition winning over rigorous analysis and critical thinking.

However, there are some situations in which intuition or instincts produce remarkable results. Often, science cannot explain those results. For example, before one of my children was diagnosed with a severe food allergy to kiwi fruit at a young age, she instinctively refused to touch the fruit on several occasions. Being exposed to even small particles of the fruit could have led to life-threatening anaphylactic shock. Some form of instinct warned her not to expose herself to the allergen.

There are many convincing examples of intuition leading to positive decisions or anticipation of future risks. Many involve animals anticipating approaching natural catastrophes. In the black belt classes these examples are analyzed and strategies contemplated.

I hope that the selection of black belt classes discussed in this chapter has caught your interest and motivated you to pursue your journey to become a black belt critical thinker. In the meantime, practice the concepts, ideas, and frameworks of critical thinking outlined in this book. They are an important and necessary foundation for future black belt classes.

CHAPTER 10: CONCLUSION AND NEXT STEPS

I sincerely hope that the ideas, concepts, tools, and frameworks presented will help you to improve your critical thinking skills and to become more successful.

Critical thinking is a skill that is acquired as are martial arts: practice, reflection, modification, and repetition. Just reading a book will not unlock the complete success potential that awaits you. You must practice the techniques and tools on a daily basis.

Becoming a critical thinker will be a dramatic change in your interactions and communication. Critical thinkers are not always welcomed with great enthusiasm. Sales people are annoyed by critical thinkers who make getting customers' business more difficult. Sales people love uncritical thinkers to whom they can present their sales pitches without encountering meaningful resistance.

Critical thinkers are of a different caliber. They do not let others push them around, manipulate them, or take advantage of them. They think for themselves and challenge unproven arguments and statements. Critical thinkers base their material decisions on rigorous analyses and facts. As a result, the quality of their decision making improves significantly. And in the long run, better decisions lead to better life outcomes.

It is your choice whether you want to please others and avoid occasional friction and confrontation but achieve poor results or chose the path of a critical thinker who may run into arguments and confrontation but has a greater chance of becoming an admired outperformer.[59]

Becoming a critical thinker will change your life. Change is often cumbersome and difficult, requiring hard work. However, it is usually the only way to achieve consistently better outcomes. Think about the following saying when reflecting on the need to change:

"If you always do,

What you always did,

You will always get,

What you always got."[60]

For most of us it would be quite frustrating and disappointing to get stuck with *"you will always get what you always got."* The risk of ending up with such an unappealing future should unleash enough energy and motivation to pursue a black belt in critical thinking and make it a cornerstone of your conduct.

After reading this book, I recommend that you reread it again with a notebook and pen in hand. Take detailed notes on three different topics:

- Negative outcomes in your life that could have been avoided by the implementation of a concept discussed here,
- Positive outcomes (yours or others) that are a result of applying a concept discussed in this book,
- Ideas of how, why, and when you should implement a concept discussed here to achieve better outcomes in the future.

I thank you again for reading this book. Please feel free to share your thoughts and experiences with me at the following email address:

successthroughcriticalthinking@yahoo.com

I look forward to hearing from you.

Good luck on your journey to become a black belt critical thinker and, of more importance, to achieve your ambitious and meaningful goals.

FOOTNOTES

---

[1] We will discuss some of the ideas of the great thinkers in *Success Through Critical Thinking Part II*.

[2] Maoshing Ni; Cathy McNease: *The Tao of Nutrition*, p.5.

[3] For example, you find a discussion of Popper in George Soros (1998): p. 29-31.

[4] Those hedge fund managers are superbly described in the book *The Big Short* by Michael Lewis (2010).

[5] BBC World Services Website, accessed July 13, 2017.

[6] Tense atmospheres often emerge when critical thinkers challenge superficial analysis conducted by others. A good joke can help to relax the situation and to reduce the tension.

[7] Wikipedia, Dick Fosbury entry, accessed September 1, 2017. This case example is based on the same source.

[8] The fight or flight response framework was first described by Walter Bradford Cannon (Wikipedia accessed March 22, 2019).

[9] Wikipedia, Greed entry, accessed July 14, 2017.

[10] State of the Union Address by President Coolidge, December 1928.

[11] Allen (1931): Only Yesterday, p.252.

[12] Not only did the German team win the 2014 World Cup, it was also the first European team ever to win a World Cup tournament in South America. The team was the most consistent performer between 2006 and 2014 as it reached the semifinal stage at each World Cup and Euro Cup tournament.

[13] Wikipedia, "Thinking outside the box," accessed September 16, 2018.

[14] Wolfgang Hammes, "What CEOs can learn from the German National Soccer Team." Unpublished Client Case Study, Boca Raton, 2014.

[15] While the fitness coaches were experts in sports science, they had limited experience in the field of soccer.

[16] Some media reports claimed that the resort was built specifically for the German soccer team. A soccer pitch was erected close by.

[17] It is worthwhile mentioning that team leadership seems to have missed this source of competitive advantage during the 2018 World Cup, which ended disastrously for the German team. They went back to traditional lodging in a suboptimal environment, a decision that was later criticized by some participants and experts.

[18] Banks were often required to keep the riskiest parts of the loan packages on their balance sheets. Over time, these highly risky slices of bundled loans created tremendous risk exposures.

[19] As I use such techniques regularly, I have covered my office walls with dry-erase boards, excellent for such types of analyses. I recommend such office design features to clients.

[20] See Joel Fuhrman (2011), *Eat To Live*.

[21] For example: The Gospel according to Matthew (24: 32-51) contains a powerful reminder of the importance of preparedness. When I grew up in Germany, I received a daily reminder of this Biblical passage on my way to school. An inscription on the highest tower of the famous Trier Cathedral cites a well-known sentence from the gospel: "Nescitis qua hora dominus veniet" (Matthew 24: 42). It reminds passersby to be prepared at all times as we do not know when the Lord will arrive.

[22] Note that all seven factors are incompatible with the requirements of critical thinking.

[23] As I pointed out in my book *The Return of High Inflation*, governmental inflation statistics often underestimate (or sometimes even ignore) the implication of the sixty percent world on inflation rates (e.g., extra costs caused by shorter product life cycles or more frequent repairs).

[24] The *Fight or Flight concept* was first described by Walter Bradford Cannon (Wikipedia, accessed on June 20, 2018).

[25] I witnessed this during the Financial Crisis of 2007. A very large number of management actions during those times fit into *fight and flight* categories.

[26] We will later learn about the 60-100-85 concept, which is based on this exercise.

[27] Loomis (2012), page 9.

[28] For a more detailed discussion on this topic see Hammes (2016): *The Return of High Inflation*.

[29] In this context, I refer to Apple's corporate history after the re-entry of founder Steve Jobs in September of 1997.

[30] While Apple has mastered all three pillars of *Total Strategic Preparedness*, we need to remind ourselves that current success is the biggest threat to future preparedness. Past success breeds behavioral traits that undermine future preparedness (e.g., laziness, overconfidence, arrogance, analytical and cognitive sloppiness). Therefore, it will be interesting to observe Apple's ongoing compliance with the requirements of *Total Strategic Preparedness*. Past success is no guarantee for future success.

[31] During the 1980s and 1990s, foreign competitors thought that they could push the German supermarkets and grocery chains out of their home markets. They failed to realize that the German grocery chains were incredibly well-managed and highly efficient. Foreign competitors retreated from the German market. In return, the poor performance of the foreign competitors encouraged the German grocery chains to attack the home markets of the foreign attackers. The German companies did so with great success. For example, Aldi has grown its market share in the U.S. and the U.K. at an impressive rate.

[32] An earlier version appeared in Hammes (2016): *The Return of High Inflation*.

[33] Wikipedia, accessed June 30, 2018.

[34] The sample consists of average performers. The results are based on either direct observations or interviews.

[35] Internet research. A similar quote is also contributed to Albert Einstein.

[36] Adam Grant, TED, April 26, 2016: *The Surprising Habits of Original Thinkers*.

[37] When threatened, the sugar cane toad excretes a toxic substance, seriously injuring or even killing animals (e.g., dogs) that lick or bite the toad.

[38] "Risky debt may cause trouble for US banks," *Financial Times*, February 20, 2000.

[39] Primary and secondary socialization are terms used in sociology to describe the processes that occur when a young child is introduced to its social environment (primary socialization) and when a person adopts a functional task (profession) in society (secondary socialization).

[40] This concept is discussed in a previous chapter of this book and is repeated to explain irrationality.

[41] Wikipedia, *Confirmation bias*, accessed July 3, 2017.

[42] It is not uncommon for German motorcycles produced in the 1970s and 1980s to be operating reliably today.

[43] These years refer to the peaks of the bubbles.

[44] *This Time is Different* is a remarkable book by Carmen Reinhard and Kenneth Rogoff (2009). It describes the history of financial crises.

[45] The PE ratio relates earnings of a company to its market price. The chart shows a version of PE ratios called CAPE ratio. It was created by Professor Robert Shiller. Quite simplified, Shiller's CAPE ratio is based on an average of the PE ratios of previous years (eliminating extreme year to year changes).

[46] Obviously, the PE ratio is only one of many factors influencing stock market valuation. This example illustrates the workings of the patient cat strategy when dealing with irrationality. It is not an endorsement of any financial strategy or recommendation.

[47] Graph is based on data published by Professor Shiller (Yale University). Website: http://www.econ.yale.edu/~shiller/data.htm.

[48] Quoted from Investopedia.com, accessed November 15, 2018.

[49] If I learned one thing in consulting, it was the importance of detecting those who leave a meeting in a state of elevated unhappiness or strong disagreement. They are "unguided missiles" spreading negative information to all of their contacts. Therefore, it is important to use critical observation to identify those people and to clarify any issues that may have evolved.

[50] Search conducted on March 30, 2018. On the same day, a similar search on Google resulted in more than 3.5 million hits.

[51] For example, some medical conditions (e.g., allergies, diabetes) or religious affiliations may greatly impact eating preferences of an individual. Critical observation must reflect on these issues.

[52] I always admired a German manager, Berthold Beitz. He died when he was ninety-nine. He always appeared to be mentally sharp, healthy, productive, and full of energy. In a biography of Beitz, I found some information about his eating preferences. Case examples like this one proved quite helpful in my research.

[53] In my job as an investment banker, I worked closely with many top executives. I noticed first-hand the enormous differences between positive and negative CEO role models regarding nutrition and other lifestyle choices.

[54] I employed rigorous critical thinking processes to test my observations and conclusions. Eliminating false observations is important. Therefore, I also conducted focused research activities and interviewed medical professionals.

[55] Based on Wikipedia entry on Alexander Fleming, accessed April 12, 2018.

[56] Part II is scheduled to be released in 2020.

[57] The word "uncertain" in the acronym SOUND refers to being uncertain about an issue due to a lack of time to conduct sufficient analysis. SOUND people avoid making decisions without having access to relevant information or required research. Therefore, do not perceive SOUND people as indecisive or weak; it is a dangerous misperception.

[58] I always encourage individuals to create an archive notebook of their own mistakes and lessons learned. Such a compilation of mistakes can be a powerful self-improvement tool.

[59] Keep in mind that critical thinkers should always try to defuse confrontational situations. There are strategies and techniques available. Some are included in this book, while more advanced techniques are part of the black belt classes.

[60] This saying has been attributed to many different people. It was difficult to find its original source. Quoteinvestigator.com (accessed on August 24, 2018) links the quote to Jessie Potter in a speech given in 1981 in Milwaukee, Wisconsin.

BIBLIOGRAPHY

Allen, Frederick Lewis: Only Yesterday, New York, 1964, originally published 1931

De Bono, Edward, Laterales Denken (Lateral Thinking), Duesseldorf 1989

Fuhrman, Joel: Eat to live, New York 2011

Hammes, Wolfgang, The Return of High Inflation, Risks, Myths, and Opportunities, Boca Raton 2016

Hammes, Wolfgang: What CEOs What CEOs can learn from the German National Soccer Team, Unpublished Client Case Study, Boca Raton 2014

Lewis, The Big Short, New York 2010

Loomis, Carol: Tap Dancing to Work: Warren Buffett on Practically Everything, New York 2012

Nadolny, Stan: The Discovery of Slowness, 1983 Munich (Original German edition), English translation 1987 by Viking Penguin, Inc.

Ni, Maoshing; McNease, Cathy: The Tao of Nutrition, Los Angeles 2009

Reinhart, Carmen M., Rogoff, Kenneth S.: This time is different, Princeton 2009

Soros, George: The Crisis of Global Capitalism, New York 1998

ACKNOWLEDGMENTS

I have the privilege of having been taught critical thinking by many exceptional people. All of them deserve my gratitude.

First of all, my parents, grandparents, godfather, and relatives invested a great deal of time in teaching me to think on my own and challenge unproven claims and beliefs.

Second, my teachers and professors at the following schools deserve my thanks for their great efforts to further develop further my critical thinking skills: Grundschule Trier-Pallien (Germany), Friedrich-Wilhelm Gymnasium Trier (Germany), Universitaet Trier (Germany), and Clark University (U.S.A.). Too often we forget to give thanks for the hard work of our teachers who selflessly spend their lives making their students more successful. The teachers I have known are truly amazing.

Third, I would like to thank all of my colleagues in my professional career for their contribution to my professional development. In particular, I would like to thank my former colleagues at McKinsey & Company.

Special thanks are due to Julie Tamarkin and Diane Adams for the difficult task of editing this book and making it more readable. If some parts of the book are still difficult to read or unclear, it is solely the fault of the author.

Finally, I would like to thank my wife Angela and our children Claudia and Maximilian for their support and patience while I was writing this book.

Let me also thank every reader for spending time with this book. Hopefully, you will gain some valuable insights.

ABOUT THE AUTHOR

Dr. Wolfgang H. Hammes is the founder and CEO of the Hammes Performance Improvement Group LLC in Boca Raton, Florida. Dr. Hammes has been a Managing Director in Investment Banking for both Merrill Lynch and Deutsche Bank in London. He has advised clients around the world on strategy and investment banking topics. At Deutsche Bank, he was co-head of the European Financial Institutions Group, advising banking and insurance clients on M&A, capital management, strategy, and risk management topics. From 1993 to 2000, Dr. Hammes worked as a top management consultant and partner at McKinsey & Company in New York and Germany. At McKinsey, he was a leader and pioneer of the firm's strategic risk management consulting activities. In early 2000, he was one of the first experts who publicly warned of a major banking crisis in the U.S. due to deteriorating risk management standards in the financial sector.

Dr. Hammes has a doctorate degree (summa cum laude) in business administration from Trier University in Germany and an M.B.A. from Clark University in Massachusetts. He was a member of the board of trustees at Clark University, where he headed the strategy and finance, compensation, and strategic risk committees. He has authored books on inflation risks and strategic alliances. He has published many articles on strategy, finance, and risk topics. He is also an active speaker at international strategy, risk management, and finance conferences and company events in North America and Europe.

ABOUT THE HAMMES PERFORMANCE IMPROVEMENT GROUP LLC

"Starting a Renaissance in Critical Thinking"

Our mission is to help our clients experience long-term success. Critical thinking plays a crucial role in our work. By linking critical thinking with the important performance levers of strategy, risk management, and future anticipation, we create a launch pad for long-term success. We call this approach the *Four Factor Critical Thinking Success Paradigm*.

The *Four Factor Critical Thinking Success Paradigm* of the Hammes Performance Improvement Group:

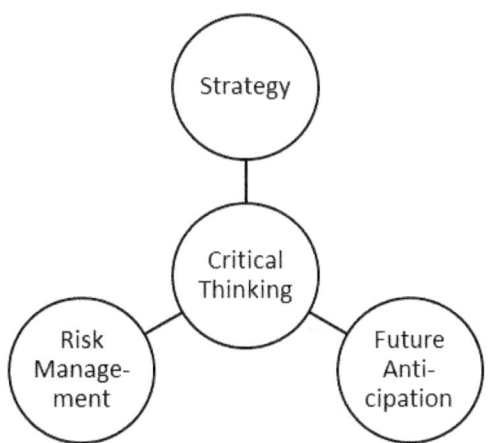

We deliver our services in multiple ways:

- Management workshops on performance improvement
- Employee workshops and training classes (e.g., "Critical Thinking for Managers")
- Consulting projects
- Publications (books, videos, newsletters, training materials, concept libraries)
- Keynote speeches

For more information, please contact us at:

info@hammesperformance.com

OTHER BOOKS BY THE AUTHOR

The Return of High Inflation: Risks, Myths, and Opportunities, Boca Raton, 2016

This book is about the next financial crisis. A crisis that, according to the author, will result from an unexpected return of high inflation and rising interest rates. The author explains the risks of such an event, describes analogies from the past, and offers numerous paradigms, concepts, and ideas that may help companies and individuals to turn inflation risks into opportunities.

Dr. Hammes was one of the first experts who foresaw the last financial crisis. As early as 2000, Dr. Hammes warned publicly that a major financial crisis was unavoidable if risk management deficiencies in the financial industry remained unaddressed. In this book, Dr. Hammes warns of an even more serious crisis caused by an unprecedented state of collective unpreparedness regarding inflation risks.

A return of high inflation to the developed world should not surprise us. Judging from historical analogies, inflation is a likely outcome of the economic malaise we are in and the policies we have chosen. Irresponsible fiscal behavior, excessive levels of government and private sector debt, and ultra-loose monetary policies are very likely to be followed by a period of excessive inflation. While we cannot precisely time the occurrence of such an inflation risk event, we can quite well assess its general probability of occurrence.

The vast majority of companies and individuals is not prepared to deal with a return of high inflation. We are in a state of collective unpreparedness. Also, there is very little practical research to help managers and individuals prepare for such a risk event. Even worse, our modern economic and financial systems and processes in the developed world are based on the assumption of low inflation. They have never been stress-tested for a different scenario.

Inflation management requires a different set of skills than those taught to us in western business schools. Reading this book should be the start of an important journey to understand better the risks of high inflation and how they impact your company and your personal life. Maybe the journey will take you one step further and enable you to turn inflation risks into a profitable opportunity as in some best practice examples during past inflation periods.

We are now at a stage in history when the economic, fiscal, financial, and social situations in many developed countries resemble terrifying parallels to past periods prior to major outbreaks of high inflation. At the moment, a wide range of inflation strategies is available to companies and individuals who take inflation risks seriously. Many of these ideas and concepts are discussed in this book. Therefore, the author's recommendation is simple: prepare for the worst and hope for the best. Do not base important risk management strategies on hope and gamble that everything will be fine. The price for being wrong is extremely high when it comes to inflation risks.

www.ingramcontent.com/pod-product-compliance
Lightning Source LLC
Chambersburg PA
CBHW071706090426
42738CB00009B/1683